MOONLIGHT AND MAGNOLIAS

BY RON HUTCHINSON

★

★

DRAMATISTS
PLAY SERVICE
INC.

MOONLIGHT AND MAGNOLIAS
Copyright © 2005, Saint Genny's Productions, Inc.

All Rights Reserved

SPECIAL NOTE

Moonlight and Magnolias was originally produced in New York City
by the Manhattan Theatre Club on March 3, 2005,
Lynn Meadow, Artistic Director; Barry Grove, Executive Producer.

The World Premiere was produced by
The Goodman Theatre, Chicago, Illinois on May 15, 2004,
Robert Falls, Artistic Director; Roche Schulfer, Executive Director.

MOONLIGHT AND MAGNOLIAS was originally produced by The Goodman Theatre (Robert Falls, Artistic Director; Roche Schulfer, Executive Director) in Chicago, Illinois, opening on May 15, 2004. It was directed by Steven Robman; the set and lighting design were by Michael Philippi; the costume design was by Birgit Rattenborg Wise; the sound design was by Richard Woodbury; the stage manager was Ellen Hay; and the production stage manager was Kimberly Osgood. The cast was as follows:

BEN HECHT .... William Dick
VICTOR FLEMING .... Rob Riley
DAVID O. SELZNICK .... Ron Orbach
MISS POPPENGHUL .... Mary Seibel

CHARACTERS

BEN HECHT

VICTOR FLEMING

DAVID O. SELZNICK

MISS POPPENGHUL

PLACE

A Hollywood studio lot, office of
legendary producer David O. Selznick.

TIME

1939.

MOONLIGHT AND MAGNOLIAS

ACT ONE

Scene 1

The lights rise on an office on a Hollywood studio lot in 1939. It's the office of legendary producer David O. Selznick. There's a cart piled high with breakfast foods in the center of the room — bagels, pastries, fruit, juices. Pink early morning Los Angeles sunlight floods in through the blinds. There are two doors leading off — one goes to the outer office, the other to the bathroom. There are two men in the room. One is Selznick himself, dressed in a sharply cut business suit, collar and tie. The other is screenwriter and playwright Ben Hecht, in casual slacks and jacket. Selznick's on his feet, looking at Hecht, who's at the cart trying to decide what to eat, dish cover in hand. Selznick looks as if he's just had some very bad news —

SELZNICK. You didn't read it?
BEN HECHT. No.
SELZNICK. You didn't read it?
BEN HECHT. No. *(Selznick thinks for a moment, tries again.)*
SELZNICK. You didn't read the book?
BEN HECHT. No.
SELZNICK. You didn't read the book?
BEN HECHT. No.
SELZNICK. You know what book I'm talking about?
BEN HECHT. Yes.
SELZNICK. This book? *(He grabs a thick volume of* Gone with the

Wind *from a shelf.*)
BEN HECHT. I didn't read it.
SELZNICK. Then what are you doing here?
BEN HECHT. You said you needed me.
SELZNICK. I need you to read the book.
BEN HECHT. Okay — *(He sets the dish cover down, takes the book, curls up in the armchair, as if settling down for a long read.)*
SELZNICK. What are you doing?
BEN HECHT. Reading the book.
SELZNICK. You're reading the book?
BEN HECHT. Yes.
SELZNICK. You don't have time to read the book. *(He snatches it back, then grins, relieved.)* You're putting me on, right?
BEN HECHT. No.
SELZNICK. It's a gag.
BEN HECHT. No.
SELZNICK. Everybody in the world has read the book.
BEN HECHT. Not me.
SELZNICK. You *know* about the book?
BEN HECHT. *Gone with the —* ? Sure. I read the first page. Feh.
SELZNICK. *Feh —* ?
BEN HECHT. Moonlight and magnolias? Gimme a break.
SELZNICK. You know why you're here?
BEN HECHT. You have a screenplay problem, you need the dialogue punched up, some character stuff fixed? Why else would you call me in?
SELZNICK. I need a whole new scenario.
BEN HECHT. You've been shooting for three weeks.
SELZNICK. I closed production down.
BEN HECHT. You did what?
SELZNICK. I'm not shooting another foot of film until I have a scenario I can believe in.
BEN HECHT. You closed down the biggest movie in Hollywood history?
SELZNICK. I'm in debt up to here, I could lose the studio, my kids' college tuition, the house — *(He presses the intercom, speaks to his assistant, Miss Poppenghul, in the outer office.)* Miss Poppenghul — ?
BEN HECHT. You went into production without a screenplay?
SELZNICK. I thought I had a screenplay. I've been working on it for three years — *(Miss Poppenghul enters.)*

MISS POPPENGHUL. Yes, Mr. Selznick?

SELZNICK. Is Fleming on the lot yet?

MISS POPPENGHUL. No, Mr. Selznick.

SELZNICK. We sent the car for him, right?

MISS POPPENGHUL. Yes, Mr. Selznick.

SELZNICK. The studio car?

MISS POPPENGHUL. Yes, Mr. Selznick.

SELZNICK. And he's not here yet?

MISS POPPENGHUL. No, Mr. Selznick.

SELZNICK. Did it get there?

MISS POPPENGHUL. Thirty minutes ago, I checked personally.

SELZNICK. With a phone call?

MISS POPPENGHUL. Yes, Mr. Selznick.

SELZNICK. That you made yourself?

MISS POPPENGHUL. Yes, Mr. Selznick.

SELZNICK. To his house?

MISS POPPENGHUL. Yes, Mr. Selznick.

SELZNICK. Where he lives?

MISS POPPENGHUL. Yes, Mr. Selznick.

SELZNICK. I want him in here the moment he arrives.

MISS POPPENGHUL. Yes, Mr. Selznick. *(She leaves.)*

BEN HECHT. Does Cukor agree with closing the movie down?

SELZNICK. George Cukor is no longer the director of *Gone with the Wind.*

BEN HECHT. You fired him?

SELZNICK. Last night. It's my studio, my picture, I can do any damn thing I want —

BEN HECHT. He's your best friend.

SELZNICK. You think that made it any easier?

BEN HECHT. Your kids call him Uncle George.

SELZNICK. Thank you.

BEN HECHT. *Uncle George.*

SELZNICK. *(Warning.)* Ben —

BEN HECHT. Mayer okayed this?

SELZNICK. Louis B. Mayer has only fifty percent of this picture. I'm in creative control. He gets half the profits, I get all the ulcers.

BEN HECHT. But you don't have a screenplay?

SELZNICK. I have you.

BEN HECHT. I didn't read the —

SELZNICK. Don't keep saying that — *(Agonized.)* You *didn't read the* — You're the only person on the face of the planet — *(His fists* bunch.) *I read the first* — *(He controls himself)* — This novel — for your information — is the biggest sensation in publishing history. It's about a nation torn in two, an entire civilization having to decide between the modern world and its past. The heroine is Scarlett O'Hara, which I can't believe you don't know, considering I've been searching for an actress to play her for the last couple of years — *(Remembering something.)* Twenty seconds — *(He presses the intercom again —)*

MISS POPPENGHUL. Yes, Mr. Selznick?

SELZNICK. Memo to Wardrobe. I'm not happy with Miss Leigh's red dress. She's got a pair of boobs, let's make sure we can get a look at them. More cleavage —

MISS POPPENGHUL. More cleavage, yes, Mr. Selznick.

SELZNICK. Any sign of Fleming yet?

MISS POPPENGHUL. No, Mr. Selznick. *(Selznick turns back to Hecht, reverently holding the book, tries to get back onto track —)*

SELZNICK. Scarlett — yes? — fights to rebuild Tara, just as the readers had to find a way to keep going through the Depression —

BEN HECHT. Tara? *(The intercom buzzer sounds —)*

MISS POPPENGHUL. Hedda Hopper on line one, Mr. Selznick — *(Selznick grabs the phone —)*

SELZNICK. No, Hedda, I have not closed production down — I don't know where you're getting your information from — *(It buzzes again —)*

MISS POPPENGHUL. Louella Parsons on line two, Mr. Selznick — *(He grabs another phone —)*

SELZNICK. That's the most ridiculous thing I ever heard — close down *Gone with the Wind* after three weeks? *(The intercom buzzes again —)*

MISS POPPENGHUL. Ed Sullivan on line one, Mr. Selznick — *(He grabs the third phone —)*

SELZNICK. Trouble? On *Gone with the Wind*? You know you'd be the first person I'd call if anything like that ever happened, Sully — *(Shaken, he sets the phone down.)* I'll give you ten thousand dollars. *(Hecht is already heading towards the door.)* Twelve. Fifteen. No screenplay? — no movie. No movie? — no more Selznick studios. No more Selznick Studios? — I'm back working for my father-in-law. Ruin. Humiliation. Failure. You want that for me?

BEN HECHT. I didn't read the —

SELZNICK. Say that once more — *(He makes a naked appeal to him —)* For me, Ben. Not for Mayer, not even for the movie —

8

for *me* —

BEN HECHT. One week, that's all.

SELZNICK. A week?

BEN HECHT. That's all I can give you.

SELZNICK. *(Disbelieving.) Ben* —

BEN HECHT. One week — you're not the only one with deadlines. *(Hecht turns back from the door, heads towards the food cart.)*

SELZNICK. Where are you going?

BEN HECHT. Breakfast?

SELZNICK. You don't have time.

BEN HECHT. It's six in the morning.

SELZNICK. I'm paying you to write, not eat. I need your total concentration here. *(He throws open the door to the outer office —) Fleming* — *(He slams it shut, pushes Hecht back into his chair —)* Now as everybody on God's Good Green Earth but you knows *Gone with the Wind* takes place during the Civil War —

BEN HECHT. There's your first problem. No Civil War movie ever made a dime —

SELZNICK. It's going to pit brother against brother, father against son —

BEN HECHT. Or ever will —

SELZNICK. *(Resisting panic.)* Okay okay … Follow me here. Overture. Front credits. Fade in on Tara.

BEN HECHT. Sure. Tara?

SELZNICK. The O'Hara's plantation in Georgia — think pillars, staircase, cotton fields, Ol' Man River — hot, it's so hot, it's always hot. *(Without warning he grabs Hecht by the lapels —)* Ah bejaysus — land, land, land — 'tis the only thing that lasts — d'you hear me? — *land* — *(Hecht pulls back in alarm —)*

BEN HECHT. David — ?

SELZNICK. Gerald O'Hara. Scarlett's father. *(Selznick sucks in his stomach, pulls himself upright, assuming Ellen O'Hara's character, using a French accent.)* — Her mother. Ellen Robillard O'Hara, mistress of Tara, *tres aristocratique, tres elegante* — *(He parades up and down, hand thrown out on limp wrist to demonstrate Ellen's character.)*

BEN HECHT. *(Wincing.) Tres* early in the day for this — *(Selznick's getting in the groove —)*

SELZNICK. Her mother's the only person that Scarlett O'Hara has ever been afraid of — *(He strikes a coquettish pose, legs crossed, hip thrown out, finger on cheek —)* Scarlett herself, beautiful, spoiled, tiny feet, flawless skin, a laugh that cares for no one — *(He leans at an exaggerated angle against the couch, tosses an imaginary mane of red hair back, whispers languorously —) Why, fiddle de dee —*

BEN HECHT. Oy — *(Selznick pulls himself upright again —)*

SELZNICK. The men. Think spurs, boots, buttons, cravats — *(He circles an imaginary enemy, jabbing and weaving —)* Every one of them desperately in love with Scarlett — yes? — who has nothing in her pretty little head but dreamy old Ashley Wilkes.

BEN HECHT. Ashley? *(Selznick sits at his desk, strikes a pose over a book —)*

SELZNICK. Proud, cultured, Mozart, Europe, books, the oboe, mezzotint — *(Hecht gets the idea —)*

SELZNICK and HECHT. No spurs —

SELZNICK. You get the main characters? *(As he explains the narrative he indicates the position on stage each of the characters he's summoning up —)* When the movie opens Scarlett's convinced that Ashley is about to declare his love for her. Then she discovers that Ashley is about to marry Melanie Hamilton, his own cousin —

BEN HECHT. Is that legal?

SELZNICK. It's the South. Scarlett has always been sure that Ashley will one day be hers. When she hears the news she assumes it's a mistake, a terrible, terrible mistake. She thinks he's going to elope with her. He says: *It can't be.* Nobody's ever said *no* to her before. She argues. *It can be.* It can't be. *It can be.* It can't be. *It can be* —

BEN HECHT. I get the idea.

SELZNICK. You're going to love this — Ashley leaves but unknown to either of them, the ruthless but charming — *(He ducks behind the couch —)* Rhett Butler — *(He jumps up again —)* has heard it all.

BEN HECHT. Rhett Butler?

SELZNICK. Think — think — think Clark Gable, that's all you have to think — She's mad at him for eavesdropping but he laughs in her face —

BEN HECHT. *Ha?*

SELZNICK. *Ha ha. (Scarlett has met her match.)* It gets even better — Stung by Ashley's rejection she marries Charles Hamilton — Melanie's brother and a poor boob who just happens to be the first person she sees after getting the heave-ho from Ashley, who's far too noble to walk out on Melanie even though we suspect he has the hots for Scarlett who in short order has a child by him —

BEN HECHT. By Ashcroft?

SELZNICK. *Ashley.* By Hamilton. But don't worry about him.

He's just about to get himself killed —

BEN HECHT. The war's broken out by now?

SELZNICK. Can't you keep up? *(He hands him a huge sheaf of papers —)* Here's Sidney Howard's scenario — most of the story beats are in there —

BEN HECHT. Most?

SELZNICK. We left a few things out.

BEN HECHT. David — this is longer than a whore's dream — *(A knock on the door.)*

SELZNICK. Yes? *(Miss Poppenghul enters —)*

MISS POPPENGHUL. Mr. Fleming, Mr. Selznick — *(Vic Fleming blows in. He's burly, physically imposing, filled with the same tightly wound energy of the others. He hovers in the doorway, anxious to leave already —)*

VIC FLEMING. I hate to kiss and run, David, whatever this is about but I have to get back to *The Wizard of Oz* set. I have a hundred and sixteen munchkins dead drunk in the corridors or fornicating in the urinals of the Culver Hotel.

SELZNICK. You're not shooting *Wizard of Oz* any more.

VIC FLEMING. I've got two weeks to go.

SELZNICK. You're through with it.

VIC FLEMING. I'm being fired? For what? Because I slapped Judy Garland around that time —

BEN HECHT. You hit Judy Garland?

VIC FLEMING. Once. *(Miss Poppenghul gasps.)* Once.

SELZNICK. We're pulling you off *Oz*, putting you onto *Gone with the Wind*.

VIC FLEMING. Cukor's shooting that.

BEN HECHT. He fired Cukor.

SELZNICK. *(Automatic.)* That's a damn lie, I don't know where these rumors start — *(Adjusting.)* Okay, yes, I did —

MISS POPPENGHUL. Shall we keep the studio car waiting for Mr. Fleming, Mr. Selznick?

SELZNICK. No.

MISS POPPENGHUL. Mr. Hecht's car?

SELZNICK. No.

MISS POPPENGHUL. Very good, Mr. Selznick. *(She closes the door with a sour look at Fleming.)*

SELZNICK. Cukor took five days to shoot the opening scene. His pacing's too slow. He's putting his own dialogue in. Margaret Mitchell's original name for Scarlett O'Hara was Pansy. That's how he's shot the movie. Pansified. I know that won't happen with you. You may be a son of a bitch bastard —

VIC FLEMING. Thanks —

SELZNICK. But you're a talented one — and Gable's a pal of yours, isn't he?

VIC FLEMING. Are you kidding? I taught him to *be* Gable.

BEN HECHT. So what happens on *Oz?*

SELZNICK. *(Dismissive.)* That's not your problem.

VIC FLEMING. It's my movie.

SELZNICK. It *was* your movie.

VIC FLEMING. So I don't have to go back to the munchkins?

SELZNICK. No.

VIC FLEMING. I can live with that. When we screened the dailies yesterday the little bastards were singing, "Ding dong the bitch is dead." *(Cautious.)* Mayer's happy with this?

SELZNICK. He agrees with me you're the only guy who could take this on.

VIC FLEMING. So give me a couple of weeks to read the screenplay, make notes, work with the actors —

SELZNICK. We don't have a couple of weeks and we don't have a screenplay. *(Hecht smiles, waves at Fleming —)*

BEN HECHT. Hi.

SELZNICK. That's why Ben Hecht's here.

VIC FLEMING. You don't have — ?

BEN HECHT. He fired the screenplay's ass, too.

VIC FLEMING. So what are we working from?

SELZNICK. You read the book?

VIC FLEMING. *(Cautious.)* It's a very big book —

SELZNICK. But you know what's in there?

VIC FLEMING. Don't most people?

SELZNICK. Not our screenwriter.

VIC FLEMING. *(To Hecht.)* You didn't — ?

BEN HECHT. No.

SELZNICK. It's not a problem. He's going to give it a week.

VIC FLEMING. A week?

SELZNICK. Seven days.

BEN HECHT. Five days. A *working* week. *(Fleming sees a copy of the book, hefts it —)*

VIC FLEMING. Five days to turn this into a screenplay?

SELZNICK. Ben can do more in five days than anybody in Hollywood.

VIC FLEMING. He's going to turn a thousand and thirty-seven pages into a hundred and thirty — ?

SELZNICK. He's the best there is.

VIC FLEMING. When he hasn't read any of them?

BEN HECHT. I read the first page.

VIC FLEMING. And?

BEN HECHT. Feh.

VIC FLEMING. David — *uh-oh* — big book — big movie —

SELZNICK. Ben wrote *Scarface* in eleven days.

BEN HECHT. *Hurricane* in two days —

VIC FLEMING. This isn't a piece of shit like those —

BEN HECHT. Piece of shit?

VIC FLEMING. You know what I mean —

BEN HECHT. That they didn't reach the giddy artistic heights of *Test Pilot*?

VIC FLEMING. There was something wrong with *Test Pilot*? *(He's shaping up physically to Hecht. Selznick hastily intervenes —)*

SELZNICK. Such kidders — The best rewrite guy in Hollywood — the only director with the balls to take this on — Big book, yes, but Ben's got Sidney Howard's first pass, he's going to work from that.

VIC FLEMING. Okay, so let me know when we have a screenplay — *(He's heading towards the door. Selznick stops him leaving —)*

SELZNICK. I need you here. There might be some things he wants to bounce off his director —

BEN HECHT. I can think of one or two things already —

SELZNICK. You're my guys. I'm your guy. That's the only way we're going to get through it. But the clock's ticking. It's costing me fifty thousand dollars a day to idle the picture. *(He thrusts a legal pad and pencil at Hecht.)*

BEN HECHT. Why doesn't Mayer re-write the movie? He called me in once. He said, "This is all you need to know about screenwriting. The rose is here. *(He holds the pencil aloft —)* It should be here." *(He moves it several inches away, shrugs.)* I'm still trying to figure what he meant. *(The good soldier and honest craftsman, he hunkers down, ready to write the story beats on the legal pad —)* So — Hamilton buys the farm and — ?

SELZNICK. The war heats up. The South attacks — *(He rushes to the other side of the room —)* The North counterattacks — *(He rushes to the opposite corner —)* The South is thrown back — *(He rushes to the first corner —)* They attack again — *(He rushes to the opposite corner —)* Once more the North counterattacks —

BEN HECHT. You're making me nauseous.

SELZNICK. Atlanta burns — *(To Fleming.)* which I shot already so you don't have to bother with that.

VIC FLEMING. Before we get into this, David — I get to finish this job, yes? It's not going to be — seven in the morning *Oz*, eight o'clock *Gone with the Wind*, nine o'clock *The Ice Follies*?

SELZNICK. I won't dignify that with an answer. *(He thrusts the script to Fleming, who tries to follow along as Selznick narrates for Hecht's benefit —)* Flames, falling buildings, people rushing here and there and in the middle of it — Oh — *(He sticks his stomach out and puts his hand on it —)* Melanie's about to have Ashley's baby. Horse, cart, Scarlett, Melanie, her baby, gunshots, looters, flames, smoke — Scarlett makes her way back to Tara — *(Selznick turns back to Hecht and Fleming, sweeping across the room, arms outstretched, as Scarlett —)* Tara, Tara, if only I can get to Tara —

VIC FLEMING. *(Screenplay in hand.)* When she gets there — mother dead — *(Selznick helpfully pulls himself into Ellen's shape —)* Father out of his mind with grief — *(Selznick sketches a crazed Gerald —)* Most of the slaves have run away — no food or livestock left, none of the neighbors has a roof over their head —

BEN HECHT. Where else would you put a roof?

SELZNICK. Scarlett finds a Union soldier looting the house — *(He mimes a struggle with Fleming —)* She's a helpless woman, alone — *(Selznick mimes a gun, aims at Fleming —)* She shoots him stone dead — *(To Fleming.)* Whatever else it is, it's a melodrama, remember that — *(Back to Hecht.)* She buries the body. She leaves Melanie and her baby at the house with a couple of loyal slaves —

BEN HECHT. *Loyal* slaves?

VIC FLEMING. She goes back to Atlanta —

BEN HECHT. I thought she just left Atlanta?

SELZNICK. In Atlanta she comes across who else but —

VIC FLEMING. Rhett Butler.

SELZNICK. He's in jail —

BEN HECHT. For impersonating Clark Gable?

SELZNICK. Scarlett is desperate for money. *(He sits on the couch alongside Fleming, tugs his jacket open —)* She offers to become Rhett's mistress if he gives it to her. He laughs in her face.

BEN HECHT. *Ha ha?*

SELZNICK. Humiliated, Scarlett marries —

VIC FLEMING. Frank Kennedy —

BEN HECHT. Did I miss him?

SELZNICK. He owns a store. She doesn't love him but she never wants to be hungry again.

BEN HECHT. Who does? *(Heading towards the breakfast cart —)* Which reminds me —

SELZNICK. Get away from the food.

BEN HECHT. Just one bagel —

VIC FLEMING. Isn't this where Scarlett sees there's money in sawmills?

SELZNICK. It's Reconstruction.

BEN HECHT. The war's over?

SELZNICK. The South will rise again — but they'll need lumber —

BEN HECHT. Lumber, yes —

VIC FLEMING. Rhett's back on the scene —

BEN HECHT. He got out of jail?

SELZNICK. He's still bewitched by Scarlett —

BEN HECHT. Who's got all that lumber —

SELZNICK. She has another baby —

BEN HECHT. Number two?

SELZNICK. It's a girl, her husband thinks it'll make her settle down —

BEN HECHT. But once a woman has discovered the lure of running a sawmill —

SELZNICK. Scarlett's attacked. Scarlett's husband and Ashley join a Klan raid to avenge her.

VIC FLEMING. Rhett saves the day —

BEN HECHT. *That* Klan?

VIC FLEMING. Aren't you following this?

BEN HECHT. The — ? *(He makes a pointed shape over his head —)* And the — ? *(He makes eye slits with his fingers —)* And especially the — ? *(He puts his hand to his throat, drops his head on one side, as if he's been lynched.)*

SELZNICK. Yes.

VIC FLEMING. Can we get on?

BEN HECHT. Hold it. *Please.* This is insane. You have a heroine whose lack of morals would be remarked on in a two-dollar whorehouse, a hero who would shoot his own grandmother in the belly, a plot that makes *Finnegan's Wake* a model of lucidity. You have this other character, Ashworthy —

SELZNICK and FLEMING. Ashley —

BEN HECHT. Who's some kind of faggot —

SELZNICK. Ashley Wilkes is not a faggot.

BEN HECHT. Played by?

SELZNICK. Leslie Howard.

BEN HECHT. An English actor? I rest my case.

VIC FLEMING. He's actually a Hungarian Jew —

BEN HECHT. He *plays* English.

SELZNICK. Ashley wants to do the right thing —

BEN HECHT. He wants to get in the little tramp's pants —

SELZNICK. *Gone with the Wind* contains one of the great love triangles of all time —

BEN HECHT. David, I don't know whether this is a very good bad book or a very bad good book or more likely a bad bad book but I do know you'll never get a movie out of it — *(Selznick pulls the door open, indicates the brass plate on it —)*

SELZNICK. David O. Selznick. *Producer. (He slams it shut again.)*

BEN HECHT. You're a great filmmaker, nobody's going to argue about that — *(He indicates the contents of Selznick's bookshelf —) David Copperfield, The Prisoner of Zenda, A Tale of Two Cities —* there isn't a classic you haven't pillaged — What happened? How did you get suckered into buying this side of lox? *(Selznick pulls some of the trades from the shelf —)*

SELZNICK. The whole world cares about this book — this movie — *(He reads some of the headlines —) Tatt av Vinden — Via Col Vento — Vom Winde Verweht — Kaze To Tomo Ni Sarinu —*

BEN HECHT. There's going to be war in Europe sometime soon.

SELZNICK. Europe's a long way away and it's none of our business.

BEN HECHT. No? With half the directors in Hollywood here because they've had to run from the Nazis? But of course you're the guy who won't give me one lousy dollar for Jewish relief —

SELZNICK. Don't start that stuff again. We have a job to do.

VIC FLEMING. *(Needling.)* And when are we going to — you know — get some — *(He mimes typing.)*

SELZNICK. I believe in this movie.

BEN HECHT. Enough to lose everything? *(He indicates the buildings and the offices outside the windows —)* The big house across the street from the Chaplins, the cars, the yacht? Your reputation as someone who's almost as smart as Thalberg was?

SELZNICK. Almost?

BEN HECHT. You really want to end up like your old man?

SELZNICK. *(Ignores it.)* You want to get to work? *(He sees Fleming about to take something from the food cart —)* Put that down — *(He grabs it —)* The digestive juices get mixed up with the creative ones. It's a scientific fact. We're going to be writing against the clock —

BEN HECHT. I've done that before.

SELZNICK. Not with these stakes.

BEN HECHT. I don't need a steak, just a bagel — *(He approaches the cart but Selznick shields it from him —)*

SELZNICK. No —

BEN HECHT. One bagel.

SELZNICK. It'll slow you down.

BEN HECHT. I'll go easy on the schmeer.

SELZNICK. I can't allow it.

BEN HECHT. Half a bagel.

SELZNICK. I can't risk it. *(Selznick opens the door — re the food cart.)* Get this out of here —

MISS POPPENGHUL. Yes, Mr. Selznick — *(Miss Poppenghul exits as Hecht turns to Fleming —)*

BEN HECHT. Tell him he's crazy.

VIC FLEMING. If you can write it, I can shoot it.

BEN HECHT. The politics of it? At a time like this?

VIC FLEMING. You're confusing me with somebody who gives a shit. *(Selznick indicates one of the shelves —)*

SELZNICK. That's the attitude. There's some production design and costume stuff there. You should try to get a jump on it. You'll be on set, Monday.

VIC FLEMING. With a script?

SELZNICK. Sure, with a script. Right, Ben? *(Hecht brandishes Sidney Howard's script —)*

BEN HECHT. *(Despairing.)* She goes to Atlanta, she leaves Atlanta, she goes back to Atlanta, she wants whatshisname, then she wants Rhett Butler, he leaves, he comes back, whatshisname leaves, he comes back, he wants her, he doesn't want her, she leaves Atlanta, she goes back to Atlanta, they're winning the war, they're losing the war, Rhett Butler's back, no — he's gone again, she's back in Atlanta, no, they're burning Atlanta, she leaves Atlanta — How in God's name is any sane person supposed to make sense of it?

VIC FLEMING. Yeah well — you're the — *(He mockingly copies the wave Hecht gave him earlier —) writer,* aren't you? *(He takes the drawings from the shelves and starts to leaf through them.)*

SELZNICK. *(To Hecht.)* If I could get a screenplay out of *Anna Karenina* I can get one out of this.

BEN HECHT. Have you even been to the South?

17

SELZNICK. I'm planning the premiere for Atlanta. I'll go then. *(He opens the door, indicates Miss Poppenghul should enter —)* You know what a banana is?

MISS POPPENGHUL. Yes, Mr. Selznick.

SELZNICK. The fruit?

MISS POPPENGHUL. Yes, Mr. Selznick.

SELZNICK. You know what peanuts are?

MISS POPPENGHUL. Yes, Mr. Selznick.

SELZNICK. I want bananas, lots of bananas, peanuts, get me peanuts. *(Perennially suspicious that he's surrounded by idiots, he queries her again —)* You know what I'm talking about? Bananas? Peanuts?

MISS POPPENGHUL. Yes, Mr. Selznick. Miss Leigh has asked if she can go back to England while the movie is down.

SELZNICK. *(Automatic.)* The movie is not — *(Controlling himself.)* Remind Miss Leigh she's still under contract and must remain in Los Angeles until we resume production so Mr. Olivier should keep it in his pants a little longer.

MISS POPPENGHUL. *(Her memo pad.)* ... in his pants ... *(Selznick makes sure Hecht hears him —)*

SELZNICK. By the end of this week Mr. Hecht will have a completed screenplay for us. You know what a typewriter is?

MISS POPPENGHUL. A typewriter?

SELZNICK. We need a typewriter, paper, carbons, pencils, erasers, pens, ink, notepads —

BEN HECHT. Cyanide capsules?

SELZNICK. — and we need them right away —

MISS POPPENGHUL. Yes, Mr. Selznick.

SELZNICK. Don't forget those bananas. They're brain food.

MISS POPPENGHUL. Yes, Mr. Selznick.

SELZNICK. Hold all my calls.

MISS POPPENGHUL. Mr. Mayer's on line one.

SELZNICK. I can't talk to him.

MISS POPPENGHUL. Mr. Louis B. Mayer.

SELZNICK. No calls.

MISS POPPENGHUL. Your father-in-law, Mr. Mayer.

SELZNICK. I know who Louis B. Mayer is.

MISS POPPENGHUL. The father of your wife.

SELZNICK. I get that.

MISS POPPENGHUL. Your wife Irene.

SELZNICK. I know my own wife's name. *(Miss Poppenghul exits as*

18

Selznick turns to Hecht with renewed energy, indicates the office —)
Where do you want to work?

BEN HECHT. Honolulu? Before we get in too deep here — does the movie have to be set in the Civil War?

SELZNICK. Yes.

BEN HECHT. You've thought this through?

SELZNICK. Yes.

BEN HECHT. *This* civil war?

SELZNICK. We only had one so far.

BEN HECHT. Somebody once told Thalberg —

SELZNICK. *(Automatic.)* It's Thalberg — always Thalberg —

BEN HECHT. — he couldn't have a beachfront scene set in Paris because Paris isn't on the ocean. Thalberg said, "We can't cater to the handful of people who know Paris." *(Fleming looks up from the drawings —)*

VIC FLEMING. Your point being?

BEN HECHT. We play with it a little — maybe we're in the right street but knocking on the wrong door —

SELZNICK. We're stuck with the American Civil War and we're stuck with this story line and these characters. We're also going to use only the dialogue that's in the book — *(Beat —)* Sure, we may not use it in the same scenes and different characters might say the words, but they're going to be the originals —

BEN HECHT. Aren't these people fighting to keep slaves?

SELZNICK. *(Evasive.)* Slavery is a part of their world, yes —

BEN HECHT. And the audience is supposed to root for them?

SELZNICK. They will if we do our jobs right.

BEN HECHT. That doesn't — ? you know — *slavery?* The owning of one person by another?

SELZNICK. It depends how it's handled. *(Selznick presses the intercom —)* Our company motto — *(Miss Poppenghul enters, recites what she's already recited many times —)*

MISS POPPENGHUL. *Selznick Pictures Create Happy Hours.*

SELZNICK. Our credo?

MISS POPPENGHUL. *To gain the respect of the American public through quality alone has always been the single aim of Selznick Pictures. That is why they are to be found at theatres of the highest standard. That is why you feel as if you had been associating with a charming and intelligent friend, as you leave the theatre —*

BEN HECHT. Not as if you've been part of a lynch mob in the Deep South?

SELZNICK. *(Ignoring him, to Miss Poppenghul.)* Where are the bananas?

MISS POPPENGHUL. Coming right in, Mr. Selznick. *(She exits.)*

BEN HECHT. Didn't you tell me that our heroine plugs a Union soldier in the belly? Don't you think that makes her — how shall I put this — a tad unsympathetic?

SELZNICK. It depends how we shoot it. Right, Victor?

VIC FLEMING. Sure — but I need a screenplay to work from and call me crazy but a screenwriter who hasn't read the material —

SELZNICK. Material? Somewhere to start? *(Selznick gives a bitter laugh —)* I have all the material he needs — *(He pulls two boxes from the shelves, starts pulling items out at random —)* First drafts, second drafts, third drafts, polishes, notes of story meetings, scene breakdowns — You want to hear what Margaret Mitchell has to say? She suggested Groucho Marx should play Rhett Butler. *(The intercom buzzer sounds —)*

MISS POPPENGHUL. Salted, plain, roasted, shelled or unshelled, Mr. Selznick?

SELZNICK. What?

MISS POPPENGHUL. The peanuts?

SELZNICK. Peanuts, just peanuts. *(Brooding, he stares at yet another shelf, on which are ranged dozens of failed screenplays. He tosses individual scripts onto the floor as he reads the writer's names.)* Whose draft do you want? Jo Swerling — John Van Druten — Oliver H.P. Garnett — Charles MacArthur —

BEN HECHT. Charlie had a piece of this, too? *(The scripts keep flying off the shelf —)*

SELZNICK. Winston Miller — John Balderston — Michael Foster — Edwin Justus Mayer — Scott Fitzgerald —

BEN HECHT. *That* Scott Fitzgerald?

SELZNICK. He gave me two lines I could use. *(Miss Poppenghul enters, pushing a cart loaded with the typewriter, office supplies, bananas and peanuts.)*

MISS POPPENGHUL. I have everything, Mr. Selznick.

SELZNICK. The bananas?

MISS POPPENGHUL. They're here, Mr. Selznick. *(Obsessive as ever, he queries her again —)*

SELZNICK. Peanuts?

MISS POPPENGHUL. On the way, Mr. Selznick. And I think you really should speak to Mr. Mayer —

SELZNICK. *(Defeated.)* Okay, okay — *(Selznick grimaces, braces himself, then takes the call as Miss Poppenghul sets out the writing table, arranges the bananas.)* L.B. — *(He opens and closes his mouth, unable to get more than a few words in as Hecht and Fleming talk —)*

BEN HECHT. *(To Fleming.)* I heard your big pal Gable had to be strong-armed into this movie.

VIC FLEMING. He's scared stiff of the role. Everybody's got it in their head that he *is* Rhett Butler. If he blows it —

SELZNICK. *(On the phone.)* Fleming's here, yes —

BEN HECHT. Wasn't there a little — *(He wiggles his hand —)* Between him and Cukor? In a men's restroom? When he first came out to Hollywood?

VIC FLEMING. Let's not get into that, buddy. Okay?

SELZNICK. *(On the phone.)* I had Hecht come in at six —

BEN HECHT. Think you'll get on with what's-her-name?

VIC FLEMING. I imagine she'll do whatever she can to get me canned and get Gorgeous George back so if at some point I'm going to have to tell Miss Fiddle-Dee-Dee to stick the screenplay up her royal British ass, I'm ready to do it —

BEN HECHT. I guess the man who slugged Judy Garland —

VIC FLEMING. I hit her once — once —

SELZNICK. *(On the phone.)* I put them straight to work —

VIC FLEMING. The question is, can you get the script done in a week? How many are you working on right now?

BEN HECHT. The new Marx Brothers movie ... one for Warners — no — two for Warners — one for RKO — four —

SELZNICK. *(On the phone.)* They're really getting into it — *(He mops his forehead, indicates for Miss Poppenghul to pour him a glass of ice water from the tray.)*

VIC FLEMING. You can keep four screenplays in your head at one time?

BEN HECHT. You can do *Wizard of Oz* one day, *Gone with the Wind* the next? *(Fleming advances on Hecht, sticks his nose into his face —)*

VIC FLEMING. Don't worry about my direction, and I won't worry about you getting writer's cramp, sonny boy —

SELZNICK. *(Phone.)* Hecht and Fleming — *(Selznick sees the two men nose to nose, as if about to come to blows — on the phone.)* What a team — *(Thankfully he puts the phone down, takes the water, drinks. Then he holds the glass at arms length, stares at it as Miss Poppenghul exits —)* Ice cubes.

BEN HECHT. Ice cubes?

SELZNICK. They wouldn't have had ice cubes back then. In period. What would they use? Crushed ice?

VIC FLEMING. The hell with the ice cubes — we don't have a screenplay — *(He indicates the lot, seen through the window —)* What about one of those bastards in the Writers Building? How about him? The guy in the argyle sweater and corduroy pants.

BEN HECHT. *One of those bastards in the Writer's Building?*

VIC FLEMING. Yeah, one of those failed poets and college professors and dollar-a-line hacks who earn more in a week than an average Joe in a year and do nothing but bitch about it —

BEN HECHT. *Bitch?*

VIC FLEMING. How much are you getting for five days' work?

BEN HECHT. That's *your* business?

SELZNICK. Ben's worth every dollar.

VIC FLEMING. It's your money, David, but why not give somebody else a chance to butcher the script?

BEN HECHT. I'm here to butcher the book. I think we can trust you to butcher the script. *(Fleming rattles the typewriter keys again —)*

VIC FLEMING. This sound mean anything to you, pal? *(Selznick presses the intercom —)*

MISS POPPENGHUL. Yes, Mr. Selznick?

SELZNICK. Get me Security — there's a writer on the loose.

MISS POPPENGHUL. *(Intercom.)* Right away, Mr. Selznick —

SELZNICK. And a memo to Props. Crushed ice any time we see a drink in somebody's hand on camera, not ice cubes. Crushed. No cubes.

MISS POPPENGHUL. *(Intercom.)* … no cubes …

BEN HECHT. I just need to know what happens in the book — the little matter of character and narrative —

SELZNICK. It's all very simple — *(The intercom squawks —)*

SECURITY CHIEF. Security here, Mr. Selznick —

SELZNICK. There's a writer out of his bungalow. Tall guy, argyle sweater, smoking a pipe —

SECURITY CHIEF. Sweater — pipe —

SELZNICK. Find out who he is and what his story is —

SECURITY CHIEF. The story he's working on?

SELZNICK. What he thinks he's doing smoking a pipe on my dime.

SECURITY CHIEF. We're on it, Mr. Selznick —

BEN HECHT. If you had a thirty-eight you could probably wing him from here. *(Selznick turns away from the intercom, back to*

Hecht. Again he indicates where the imaginary characters have been established on the stage —)

SELZNICK. Scarlett thinks she's in love with Ashley Wilkes but he's going to marry Melanie although he's really in love with Scarlett who's in love with Rhett Butler though she doesn't know it so to spite Ashley she marries the first guy she sees and has a baby by him but he gets killed which means she's free to chase after Ashley again but she can't because by this time he's married to Melanie by which time Rhett Butler who everybody thinks doesn't love anybody but himself is in love with Scarlett.

BEN HECHT. *(Trying hard to get it.)* Okay — Scarlett thinks she's in love with — who?

VIC FLEMING. *(Explodes.)* The worst thing that happened to this business was talking pictures. Now we need "the words," we have to sit around waiting for a goddamn Chicago newspaperman to deliver —

BEN HECHT. You were a chauffeur, yes? You gave somebody a ride to a movie shoot and the camera broke down and you fixed it and now you're Mr. Big Shot Director —

VIC FLEMING. You can't pull this off, you might end up writing for the newspapers again, Mr. Rewrite Guy. *(Hecht turns an imaginary steering wheel —)*

BEN HECHT. *Toot toot toot —*

VIC FLEMING. You might end up back in the Windy City — *(Mimes shivering from the cold.) Brrr brrr brrr* — *(Selznick steps between them, pleading —)*

SELZNICK. I need this, guys. I need it. You have no idea how badly I need it. My father-in-law's just waiting for me to fall on my ass. He told Irene, "Keep away from that schnook. He'll be a bum, just like his old man." *(He's naked, desperate —)* Give me a hit, fellas. A *hit.* You know what it's like when a million people go see your movie? When a million people say *Yes? (Selznick drags Hecht to the window, looks longingly out —)* Ever been on a lot Monday morning when the studio's had a smash that weekend? Even the cop on the gate is standing a little taller. There's an extra snap in the way the waiter in the commissary opens your napkin. *Yes, sir.* Suddenly you're a genius. The fact that every previous release for the past three years has been a dog doesn't matter any more — you out of all the people in Hollywood know exactly what those Joe Blows and Jane Does want to plunk their fifty cents on; other people have hits, sure, but that's dumb luck — *you,* you genius bastard, made it happen on sheer talent and you're going to keep on doing it, week after week, movie after movie from now on, everything you touch is going to turn to gold — But it's not just the money. It's knowing that you *know.* You know what I mean — *you know?*

BEN HECHT. And they forget you're a Jewboy in English tweeds?

SELZNICK. Nix the Jewboy —

BEN HECHT. Who they won't let into their country club —

SELZNICK. Can you stay off that for five minutes?

BEN HECHT. You want to belong so badly? Fine. I'll give it my best shot. But in five days? Working from this? *(Sidney Howard's script.)* With *him? (Fleming gives a helpless shrug —)* Okay — *(He picks up the book —)* Scarlett thinks she's in love with Ashburton —

VIC FLEMING. Ashley —

SELZNICK. No. *(Selznick dumps the book into the wastebasket.)*

BEN HECHT. But he's about to marry his own sister? *(Hecht reaches for the screenplay, Selznick grabs that, too —)*

SELZNICK. No — *(He takes a deep breath —)* What's a movie? Specks of light stuck to a strip of celluloid. Did you ever think of it like that? A goddamn authentic miracle. A series of moments frozen in time by the only time machine ever invented. So what do we want our specks of light to be? This time? When we're sitting in a movie palace and the lights go down — *(He dims the lights —)* And the theater disappears and the magic starts to happen? *(He starts to open the drapes —)* Say we hear an overture — I don't know — something like — *da da da da dah dah dah da da* — and the curtains open — *da da da dah — (He opens the curtains fully —)* And on the screen we see a sky in flames, a sky that looks as if it's the end of the world — *(He holds his hand up, as if he can almost touch the image —)* Shapes, silhouettes, backs bent in toil — *da da da da da da da da* — an image of back breaking labor, endless struggle —

BEN HECHT. It's the Writer's Building?

SELZNICK. It's Tara — *(Fleming's directing instincts take over —)*

VIC FLEMING. I put the camera down here, yes, shooting up — the angle says it all — Tara fills the screen — it's not just a house — it's the entire world of the South — a whole way of life —

SELZNICK. *Tara* — you can smell the red, ripe, rotting earth, Ben — it's as red as the sky, red as the blood that beats in the hearts of a people who know their way of life is doomed but who'll spill every ounce in defense of their hopeless cause —

BEN HECHT. It *is* the Writer's Building — *(Pissed off at Hecht's attitude, Selznick's heading towards the door —)*

24

SELZNICK. Okay, that's it — *(He switches the lights back on.)*
VIC FLEMING. Silhouettes and shadows, too, lots of shadows, blacks and reds, strong colors, figures against landscape, epic —
SELZNICK. Epic, yes —
VIC FLEMING. Epic as all shit — *(Selznick opens the door as Miss Poppenghul enters with a huge bowl of peanuts —)*
SELZNICK. You know what a door is?
MISS POPPENGHUL. Yes, Mr. Selznick.
SELZNICK. You know what I mean when I say, "This door stays closed?"
MISS POPPENGHUL. Yes, Mr. Selznick.
SELZNICK. If I tell you nobody comes in here for the next five days — you know what I mean?
BEN HECHT. David —
MISS POPPENGHUL. Yes, Mr. Selznick. *(She takes out a key.)*
SELZNICK. You know what a telephone is?
MISS POPPENGHUL. Yes, Mr. Selznick.
SELZNICK. So when I say no calls for the next five days —
VIC FLEMING. *David —*
BEN HECHT. I didn't agree to this —
SELZNICK. You said you'd give me five days. *(To Fleming.)* You're on contract, remember. *(Indicating.)* There's the bathroom, there's the bananas. *(To Miss Poppenghul.)* We have peanuts too?
MISS POPPENGHUL. Yes, Mr. Selznick.
SELZNICK. The door — *(She exits.)* Big book, yes. But big brain — *(He claps Hecht on the shoulder —)* Big guy — *(He claps Fleming on the shoulder —)* Big shot — *(He sticks his thumb in his own chest —)* Five days, one screenplay. *(To Hecht.)* The blood-red sky — *(Hecht sits at the typewriter.)*
BEN HECHT. Sure, the blood red sky. Then what?
SELZNICK. Then Fleming and me act out the book for you.
VIC FLEMING. Act out the book?
SELZNICK. You have a better idea?
VIC FLEMING. The whole book? *(Selznick rearranges the furniture to create an acting area —)*
SELZNICK. We do a scene from the book, he watches it, he writes it up as a movie scene; we do the next scene, he says, "Why do we need this scene, we can tell the story without it," so we toss that scene — we look at the next scene and by the end of the week we have a movie —
BEN HECHT. *(Shrugs.)* That nobody's going to want to watch

but hey —

SELZNICK. Fade up — *(Unwilling to argue any more, Hecht starts to type —)*

BEN HECHT. *One —*

SELZNICK. *Exterior —*

BEN HECHT. *Day —*

SELZNICK. *Tara —*

VIC FLEMING. Big, it's all got to be big, the acting, the emotions, we have to ham it up, make them forget what piffle it is —

BEN HECHT. *(Impatient.)* So let's go — *(Selznick puts his hands on his hips, sashays across the room, a la Scarlett O'Hara —)*

SELZNICK. *War, war, war — that's all anybody can talk about — (He reaches Fleming.) War, war, war —*

VIC FLEMING. What?

SELZNICK. What?

VIC FLEMING. I'm not an actor —

SELZNICK. You think I am? *(Hecht is typing —)*

BEN HECHT. I'm running low on dialogue here —

SELZNICK. *War war war — (He drapes himself coquettishly on Fleming —) Why, Ashley Wilkes, I didn't see you there — (He waits for Fleming to answer — impatient.)* You do remember the book?

VIC FLEMING. Sure — ah — *(He makes an effort to recall —)* Hey — Scarlett — how's it going?

BEN HECHT. *Hey Scarlett, how's it going?*

SELZNICK. You're Ashley Wilkes, okay?

BEN HECHT. You have to give me something to work with.

VIC FLEMING. Ashley, okay, Ashley —

SELZNICK. Unless you'd rather play Scarlett?

VIC FLEMING. No, Ashley's good.

BEN HECHT. Five days and you lose me, remember. *(Fleming makes an attempt to portray Ashley —)*

VIC FLEMING. *I ... I ... I've something to say to you, Scarlett. Something to tell you about my cousin Melanie and me — (Selznick drapes himself in Fleming's arms, looking up at him with fluttering eyelashes as Hecht keeps hammering the keys —)*

SELZNICK. *Melanie? Poor little flat-chested, skinny little Melanie? (He gives a high pitched, coquettish laugh —) Why fiddle dee dee — (The lights fade with the sound of a thousand frantic typewriter keys getting louder and louder, like an army of typists at work against the clock ...)*

Scene 2

In the blackout we hear that frantic clattering of typewriter keys. As the lights rise we see the room lit by the soft glow of table and floor lamps. It's the middle of the night two days later. By the lamp light we see the devastation that's been wrought in the office since we last saw it. Scores of papers are scattered on the floor, there are heaps of banana skins and piles of peanut shells on every surface, the cardboard boxes have been overturned and the contents spilled out. It looks like a battle has taken place here — and the rumpled, dishevelled, wild-eyed state of the three men emphasize it further. They're all in shirtsleeves, their hair is wild, their chins are dark with stubble. Hecht winces as he types, as if his fingers are aching in every joint. Regardless, he hammers on, the consummate pro. Even for him it's a struggle to stay upright, gripped by fatigue and hunger. He shades his eyes as if they're hurting him, looks across the room to where Fleming is lying on the floor as Melanie, giving birth. Selznick is crouching over him, as Scarlett —

SELZNICK. *Push — push.*
VIC FLEMING. *I'm pushing —*
SELZNICK. *Push harder —*
VIC FLEMING. *Uh —*
SELZNICK. *Harder —*
VIC FLEMING. *Uh — uh —*
SELZNICK. You have to throw yourself into it —
VIC FLEMING. *Uh uh uh — (Selznick gets to his feet —)*
SELZNICK. *It's no good — where is that girl? Prissy, Prissy — (He looks at Hecht but Hecht has fallen forward on the desk, snoring gently —)* Ben — *(Hecht jerks awake —)*
BEN HECHT. Wha — ?
SELZNICK. Scarlett's in Atlanta, remember?
BEN HECHT. Atlanta?
SELZNICK. Melanie's having Ashley's baby —
BEN HECHT. Melanie?
SELZNICK. There's only Scarlett to help her —

BEN HECHT. Scarlett? *(Hecht goes to type, then winces —)* Ow —

SELZNICK. Not again — *(He goes to Hecht's desk, massages his knees as Fleming rolls over, goes to sleep. With a painful grunt Hecht manages to straighten his knees.)*

BEN HECHT. I think I lost the use of my legs — *(He leans on Selznick as he gets to his feet, still hunched forward. Selznick grabs him by the shoulders and jerks him upright.)*

SELZNICK. Have a banana. *(Hecht gives a short, shrill screech.)* Peanut? *(Hecht gives the same screech.)* Take it easy.

BEN HECHT. Goddamn you to hell, David Selznick. I haven't had a bowel movement in two days — I'm deaf in my right ear from this goddamn typewriter — *(He tugs at his pants. There's a good three-inch gap between his belt and his belly —)* I must have lost five pounds. *(He indicates his left hand. It's still twitching, typing on invisible keys.)* Look at that.

SELZNICK. It's nothing serious — *(Hecht walks a couple of shuffling steps, feels something crunching underfoot.)*

BEN HECHT. What's that?

SELZNICK. You threw the peanuts at me, remember?

BEN HECHT. *(Hopefully.)* Did I hurt you badly?

SELZNICK. Fleming held you down until you were over it.

BEN HECHT. Fleming? *(He looks vaguely towards the snoring form of Fleming —)* What's he doing here?

SELZNICK. Stop kidding around. *(He prods Fleming awake.)*

VIC FLEMING. *I'm pushing, I'm pushing —*

SELZNICK. We're doing pretty good — *(He lifts up a pile of completed script pages by the typewriter —)* We're making progress but we've still got a ways to go — *(Hecht groans, winces —)*

BEN HECHT. My back —

SELZNICK. We have to keep going —

BEN HECHT. My head —

SELZNICK. You know where we are, right? In the story?

BEN HECHT. Let me take a walk, get some fresh air — *(He takes a half-hearted trot towards the door but Selznick heads him off —)*

SELZNICK. No. *(Hecht heads towards the couch —)*

BEN HECHT. Let me sleep for ten minutes —

SELZNICK. We don't have time. *(He directs him back to the typewriter.)* We have a baby on the way here. *(Hecht looks around, dazed, as if trying to see it —)*

BEN HECHT. A baby?

SELZNICK. Melanie's having Ashley's baby with only Scarlett to help. Scarlett's maid Prissy told her she knew about birthing babies but she didn't know nu'thing. *(He leans over Fleming as Scarlett again —) Push — push — (He gets to his feet —)*

VIC FLEMING. *I'm pushing.*

SELZNICK. Prissy's taking too long — Melanie's in a real bad way —

VIC FLEMING. *Uh — uh —*

SELZNICK. Prissy comes back, dawdling — *(He indicates Fleming should get to his feet —)*

VIC FLEMING. I'm having a baby here.

SELZNICK. Not without Prissy. *(Fleming gets to his feet to play Prissy —)* Prissy runs up the stairs — *(Fleming mimes running up the stairs —)* She's alone, she hasn't brought any help, she's a bad, bad stupid girl —

VIC FLEMING. *I's a stupid stupid girl —*

SELZNICK. Scarlett loses it and — *(He slaps Fleming across the face.)* Now Scarlett's left with a woman who's giving birth to a child by the one man Scarlett ever loved —

BEN HECHT. *(Disbelieving.)* Whoa — whoa — back up —

SELZNICK. You wonder why this book sold a million and a half copies in twelve months? There it is, right there. You want to talk character, dilemma, dramatic irony? Zola couldn't have done it any better.

BEN HECHT. Hold it — *(He squeezes his forehead, trying to assemble his thoughts —)* She slaps the maid?

SELZNICK. Socks her one right here —

BEN HECHT. The colored maid?

SELZNICK. Prissy. *(Fleming mimes Prissy —)*

VIC FLEMING. *I's a stupid, stupid girl.*

BEN HECHT. How old's this girl?

SELZNICK. Ten, twelve?

BEN HECHT. You can't put this in a movie.

SELZNICK. The girl lied to her. She said she could birth babies.

VIC FLEMING. *I did, I told Miss Scarlett I could birth babies —*

SELZNICK. Then she dawdles on the way back —

VIC FLEMING. *I did, I dawdled something awful — (He skips, miming Prissy's dawdling.)*

SELZNICK. Meantime Melanie's dying here. *(Fleming hits the floor, as Melanie —)*

VIC FLEMING. Okay — push — push —

BEN HECHT. You're paying me to tell you what scenes to cut.

Cut this one.

SELZNICK. No.

BEN HECHT. Have you any idea what it says about your heroine?

SELZNICK. She's under a lot of pressure here —

BEN HECHT. So it's okay to beat up the black kid? *(Fleming drags himself to his feet again —)*

VIC FLEMING. *I know I's been a bad girl — (He skips, miming the dawdling again.)*

SELZNICK. *(To Hecht.)* Could you please dialogue-in the scene?

BEN HECHT. No.

SELZNICK. Write it.

BEN HECHT. I won't do it.

SELZNICK. Who's the producer?

BEN HECHT. Who's the writer?

VIC FLEMING. So *write.*

BEN HECHT. What happened, David? *You?* Making a movie that doesn't just glorify the Confederacy but — *she slaps the little girl?*

SELZNICK. The audience is waiting for it.

BEN HECHT. Look at how Fleming's playing Prissy.

SELZNICK. He's not an actor.

BEN HECHT. Don't you have a responsibility to make America look its ugly mug in the face?

SELZNICK. My only responsibility is to make the best movie I can.

BEN HECHT. This isn't the David Selznick I know, the David Selznick I admire, I *love* — In this gold-lined sewer I always thought there was one executive who saw things the way I do —

SELZNICK. I can't deal with the race question now.

BEN HECHT. If you can't deal with it in *Gone with the Wind,* when will you?

VIC FLEMING. Oh God — more Chicago newspaperman BS — *(Fleming heads unsteadily to the restroom.)* I'll be in the john —

BEN HECHT. If there's one person who could make this movie mean something, it's you.

SELZNICK. It's a melodrama. Possibly the greatest one ever written but a *melodrama* —

BEN HECHT. If there's anybody who can understand the legacy of prejudice it's us Jews.

SELZNICK. *(Bewildered.)* How did the Jews get into this?

BEN HECHT. *The audience is waiting for the slap?* What are you thinking?

SELZNICK. That I don't have you for much longer and Melanie's having a baby and Scarlett sees Prissy and *blam*. Where's Fleming? Write it.

BEN HECHT. Not in a million years.

SELZNICK. I've spent a lot of time, effort and money making sure everybody in this story is treated with respect —

BEN HECHT. As much as you've spent on Vivien Leigh's breast-work? On the ice cubes?

SELZNICK. The Negro characters in my movie will have as much dignity as all the other characters —

BEN HECHT. However you slice it, this is an elegy for the Old South. Tell me you see the problem. Harry Cohn wouldn't see it. Jack Warner wouldn't see it. Thalberg might have —

SELZNICK. Enough with the Thalberg — write it —

BEN HECHT. I can't write it.

SELZNICK. I have to be loyal to the book.

BEN HECHT. How about being loyal to your conscience?

SELZNICK. There's only so much I can do.

BEN HECHT. That's kind of disappointing, don't you think?

SELZNICK. *Write it. (Hecht goes to the typewriter again, energized, defiant —)*

BEN HECHT. Okay, okay — how about this? We keep the slap but we give Prissy a speech — Yes, she says, defiantly, holding her hand to her bleeding mouth, *I did dawdle, I did take my time, I know Miss Melly's hurting up there, hurting real bad — (Fleming's voice sounds from behind the closed bathroom door —)*

VIC FLEMING. *Push — push —*

BEN HECHT. *— and if she dies what do I care, because what do any of you care, any of you white folk, you in particular Miss Scarlett O'Hara, about us, the people who've made the wealth, who toiled and died for you, year after year, generation after generation —* You see where I'm going? *(He stands as he types, fired up —) I hope she dies and I hope you die, because something else is being born right now, too — a new America, where there's a place for me as well as you —*

SELZNICK. Are you nuts?

BEN HECHT. Okay, it's a first pass —

SELZNICK. Give me that — *(Before Hecht can protest he rips the paper out of the typewriter. There's a sudden cry from the restroom —)*

VIC FLEMING. *(Offstage.)* Aaaaaahh — *(Hecht and Selznick rush to the bathroom door. Offstage.)* Aaaaaaaaahh — *(It opens and Fleming stumbles out. He's clutching at his left eye.)*

SELZNICK. What is it?

VIC FLEMING. My eye —

SELZNICK. Let me see —

VIC FLEMING. You don't want to look — *(Selznick grabs his hand, looks at his eye, backs away —)*

SELZNICK. My God —

BEN HECHT. What is it?

SELZNICK. You don't want to look. *(They stare at Fleming. One of his eyeballs is bright red.)*

VIC FLEMING. Will I lose the eye?

BEN HECHT. It's only a burst blood vessel.

VIC FLEMING. *(Panicking.)* I can't work if I lose the eye.

BEN HECHT. You're not going to lose the eye. Sit down — *(He guides him to an armchair. Fleming sinks into it, grabs his hand —)*

VIC FLEMING. Don't let this get out, okay?

SELZNICK. It's nothing serious.

VIC FLEMING. I can get insured for any movie you want me to make.

SELZNICK. I want you to make this one.

BEN HECHT. Relax — *(He strokes the back of Fleming's hand, trying to soothe him —)* Breathe —

VIC FLEMING. I don't want to go back to driving somebody else's car —

SELZNICK. You won't have to do that —

BEN HECHT. Who'd employ a one-eyed driver? *(Fleming takes a half hearted swing at Hecht, falls back in the chair —)*

VIC FLEMING. You don't think I could lose the eye? *(Selznick strokes his hand again —)*

SELZNICK. Ssssshh —

VIC FLEMING. I mean, they wouldn't take out an eye because you burst a blood vessel, would they? I can still read a script — *(He feels on Hecht's desk, pulls out the new page Hecht typed, reads, with one hand over his eye, holding the page an inch from him —)* Yes, I did dawdle, I did take my time, I know Miss Melly's hurting up there, hurting real bad — and I'm glad, do you hear, I'm glad, and if she dies what do I care, because what do any of you care, any of you white folk, you in particular Miss Scarlett O'Hara — *(He stares at it in disgust —)* Where did this piece of shit come from?

SELZNICK. It's something Ben was trying out — *(He grabs the page before Hecht can retrieve it —)*

BEN HECHT. Piece of shit? *(Goading.)* Where do you stand on the race question, Mr. Fleming? Do you think there's a place for it in the popular movie?

VIC FLEMING. You're just a newspaper man at heart, aren't you, Hecht? *Brr brr brr* —

BEN HECHT. As a director you make a pretty good chauffeur. *Toot toot toot* —

VIC FLEMING. Any damn fool could write a screenplay like this. We've acted it for you. We've given you the dialogue. What more do you want?

BEN HECHT. Do you mind? David and I are trying to get some work done here —

VIC FLEMING. Do I mind? *(Fleming bristles, near breaking point —)* Do I mind? The "writer's" trying to do some "work" so I should disappear up my own ass?

SELZNICK. *Push* —

VIC FLEMING. Selznick and me are the ones who've been doing "the work," sonny boy —

SELZNICK. *Push* —

VIC FLEMING. You're maybe feeling the heat for the couple of hours it's going to take to put this piece of shit screenplay together. But where are you going to be the six months I'm going to be living with this turkey day after day, hour after hour?

SELZNICK. Here comes Prissy — *(Fleming ignores him, bears down on Hecht —)*

VIC FLEMING. Is "the writer" going to deal with set, wardrobe, props, transport, hair, make-up, catering — *him* — *(He indicates Selznick.)*

SELZNICK. She's on the stairs —

VIC FLEMING. Are you going to sit up to midnight because your actors refuse to come to work because they don't like the color of their shower curtains? Are you going to hold their hands, let them put their heads on your shoulders, listen to their life stories when all you really want to do is punch them in the nose and tell them, *it's acting, just turn up and say the line, damn it?*

BEN HECHT. In the beginning was The Word.

VIC FLEMING. But it doesn't get said unless some poor son of a bitch shouts *Action.*

BEN HECHT. *(Needling.)* If it's true that no director starts out to make a bad movie then what *is* the explanation?

VIC FLEMING. Because even before the shooting starts somebody's nagging at me — drop this scene, drop that scene, *do you really need so many extras* — Going into a production without a screen-

play's a great idea — You get to the set — Day One somebody takes you aside, there's a problem, casting, location, whatever, *can you give us a little help here, can you be flexible?* Day Two somebody else asks you to compromise on something else — You give a little bit here, a little bit there, what the hell — Say it takes nine months to get from script to premiere. Given one little compromise a day, that's two hundred and seventy compromises. Say your movie lasts ninety minutes, that's one compromise every twenty seconds.

SELZNICK. Guys, please —

BEN HECHT. *(Ignoring him.)* You want to talk about compromise? Imagine you meet this drop-dead beautiful woman and there's an unspoken "Yes" in her eyes and you say, "Your place or mine?" And when you get there she slips her shoes off and you put something slow on the Radiola and she breathes "Yes" and then you're in the bedroom and she's naked in the moonlight and there's that "Yes" in her eyes again and you're about to climb out of your pants when the director steps through the door and says "Okay, I'll take over now — leave it to me — " How'd you like to be a Hollywood screenwriter, mac? How'd you like to live with that?

VIC FLEMING. Suck it down, pal. The real movie magic is somebody like me showing up on a sound stage and turning this — *(He grabs the completed pages of the screenplay —)* into those specks of light Selznick's always bullshitting about.

SELZNICK. In the beginning was The Deal. You don't get to write the words — *(Hecht.)* You don't get to shout action — *(Fleming.)* until somebody puts the money together. Now *that's* an art form. You want to talk about being creative? — Take a look at the studio's books. That's real imagination. You're disappointed in me, Ben? It's a free country, anybody can make the movie they want. You want to make *your Gone with the Wind* — go ahead — as long as you can raise a million dollars and control the rights. You have a million dollars? You have the rights? No? Then maybe you're here to help me make the *Gone with the Wind* I want to make. I pay you to write it the way I want it written and somebody like Fleming to direct it the way I see it. That's called collaboration.

BEN HECHT. Only in Hollywood. *(Selznick reaches for the battered copy of the book —)*

SELZNICK. Movies get made because somebody like me, who everybody thinks is the asshole who just happens to own the studio, picks up a book and, sure, yes, I think it's going to be another moonlight-and-magnolias but a couple pages in the same thing

34

happens to me as happened to Margaret Mitchell. Scarlett O'Hara grabbed me by the nuts and never let go. I think Mitchell started out to write just another bodice ripper but Scarlett took the book over. You don't make judgements about the little brat. You go with her. A million and a half readers did. As sure as I know there's a God of the movies, I know that tens of millions of moviegoers will —

BEN HECHT. Who exactly might the god of the movies be? You?

VIC FLEMING. No, but he is a very close relative.

BEN HECHT. So we have to do it your way? Me — *(Indicates Fleming.)* Him?

SELZNICK. Somebody has to have the vision and willpower to make it all happen. That's just how it is.

BEN HECHT. Isn't that what Hitler's telling his people? What Mussolini and Stalin have been telling theirs?

SELZNICK. Hitler couldn't take the pressure of running a studio, Mussolini wouldn't have the patience, and Stalin's too nice — Get back to your desk —

BEN HECHT. Aren't you running a dictatorship, too?

SELZNICK. Those guys don't have Mayer breathing down their necks — I've been carrying this movie in my gut for three years. I *know* Scarlett O'Hara. I *know* Melanie. I *know* Ashley and Rhett Butler and Tara and I care about them more than any hired hand, which at the end of the day are what you two are — *(At Fleming.)* — and while we're talking about compromises the shape of the ice cubes does matter, okay, *everything* matters — one mistake and the whole illusion's lost, it's just a bunch of actors standing in front of wood and canvas — *(Beseeching.)* I can taste this movie but I need your help to get it on the screen — *(Setting the book down again.)* I raise the money — Fleming figures where the camera goes and how the actor says the line — Isn't there something you should be doing? You stop blubbering like a girl about your eye — *(Fleming.)* You stop dreaming of making Hollywood what it can never be — *(Hecht.)* Put your butt into that chair and give me Prissy's big scene — *(Hecht fits in a new page, types defiantly —)*

BEN HECHT. *Scarlett hauls off on the girl. Her head swings around like she's been hit by a baseball bat —*

SELZNICK. No —

BEN HECHT. *Scarlett's fist connects. The girl's head explodes like a ripe watermelon —*

SELZNICK. No —

BEN HECHT. *Scarlett nails her. Her jaw snaps with a twang —*

SELZNICK. No —

BEN HECHT. You see the problem?

SELZNICK. Write it, damn it —

BEN HECHT. What is it — a right hook?

VIC FLEMING. It could be an uppercut — a jab — *(He thoughtfully throws some punches —)* Does she cold-cock her? I dropped a guy in a bar once with one of these — *(He makes a sudden head butt.)*

BEN HECHT. Then a kick in the ribs?

SELZNICK. *Write it* —

BEN HECHT. Our adulterous, two-timing, slave-driving heroine is now about to add child abuse to her résumé —

SELZNICK. It's just a little slap —

BEN HECHT. Vivien Leigh's no Joe Louis but she either connects or she doesn't —

SELZNICK. *(Losing it.)* Mayer wants me to fail. All the people who said this was the biggest white elephant in Hollywood history want me to fail — all the people who, okay, said I was going to end up like my dad, losing everything he ever had — all the people who Thalberg this and Thalberg that — but I'm going to make the best damn movie this town has ever made, the best damn movie in the history of the world and I need this scene. I need it, Ben, I need it, for God's sake, I need it — *(He suddenly freezes, as if locked in position —)*

BEN HECHT. David? You okay? *(Selznick doesn't move.)* I said are you okay?

VIC FLEMING. What did you do to him?

BEN HECHT. He just kind of — froze.

VIC FLEMING. You think it's the bananas?

BEN HECHT. I don't know.

VIC FLEMING. You killed him.

BEN HECHT. Don't say that.

VIC FLEMING. Over one lousy scene.

BEN HECHT. We should call a doctor.

VIC FLEMING. Did I get one for my eye?

BEN HECHT. This is different. This is — freezing. *(Fleming leans forward, listens to Selznick's breathing —)*

VIC FLEMING. He's still breathing. *(He holds Selznick's wrist —)* He's got a pulse. *(They pull back, stare at Selznick, frozen stiff. Fleming reaches for the phone on Selznick's desk.)*

BEN HECHT. What are you doing?

VIC FLEMING. Calling a doctor.

BEN HECHT. We can call from home. *(Fleming is momentarily*

puzzled. Then he gets it. He sets the phone down. He looks at the door. Fleming follows his look.) You wouldn't like a shower, a shave, a clean shirt?

VIC FLEMING. *(Tempted.)* Something to eat — ?

BEN HECHT. Get that eye looked at —

VIC FLEMING. I could murder a rib-eye —

BEN HECHT. Take a shower —

VIC FLEMING. A short stack of blueberry pancakes —

BEN HECHT. A toasted onion bagel, light on the cream cheese, nova and a pickle — *(They head towards the still-catatonic Selznick —)*

VIC FLEMING. You can't ask people to work like this —

BEN HECHT. Lock them in a room —

VIC FLEMING. Give them peanuts and bananas — *(They rifle through his pockets, find the key of the door that leads to the outer office.)*

BEN HECHT. Look at this place —

VIC FLEMING. Have you seen the bathroom?

BEN HECHT. You don't treat the director of *Test Pilot* like this —

VIC FLEMING. The writer of *Hurricane* —

BEN HECHT. What about some respect for the guy who puts the movie on the screen?

VIC FLEMING. The guy who gives us the screenplay to work with?

BEN HECHT. The peanuts —

VIC FLEMING. The bananas —

BEN HECHT. The bathroom — *(He unlocks the door, cautiously tugs it open, peers into the outer office.)* She's not at her desk.

VIC FLEMING. In the ladies room?

BEN HECHT. *(Nods.)* We could make it to Washington Boulevard, call for a cab —

VIC FLEMING. What about the guards on the gates? Would they shoot?

BEN HECHT. Come on — *(He's about to go through the door when he sees Fleming hesitate.)* What?

VIC FLEMING. I don't know —

BEN HECHT. Selznick can't be right and the rest of the world wrong. This movie's going to derail the career of everybody involved with it. He's screwed up with the eyes of the world on him. He'll be eating crow at MGM by the end of the month.

VIC FLEMING. Hey — I'm keeping out of the family stuff. I advise you to do the same. You know what these people are like.

BEN HECHT. These people?

VIC FLEMING. The — you know —

BEN HECHT. All these Jews?

VIC FLEMING. That's not what I'm getting at —

BEN HECHT. All the Jews who run the studios?

VIC FLEMING. *(Exasperated.)* There you go again. I started out as a driver, okay, *buddy?* And every time I sit in the studio car I'm saying to myself *I'm never going to be that sucker again.*

BEN HECHT. That's the most pathetic thing I ever heard.

VIC FLEMING. Those lines are the most pathetic thing I ever heard. *(Hecht indicates the outer office, nerving himself —)*

BEN HECHT. I'm going to make a run for it.

VIC FLEMING. Nobody could blame you. A writer can work anyplace. Me? I'd rather be sitting in the limo than working under it with a wrench.

BEN HECHT. *Adios —*

VIC FLEMING. I happen to agree with you — this is a piece of shit. *(Indicates Selznick.)* He has a heroine who doesn't have enough class to be a hooker. Ashley Wilkes is a pantywaist. The rooting interest is Gable but not even Gable can pull this off. But you know what — ? *(Indicates Selznick.)* You said you'd give him five days. And if there's anybody who could figure out how to stuff this sausage, it's Ben Hecht.

BEN HECHT. The newspaperman? *Brrr brrr brrr —*

VIC FLEMING. I've seen what you can do. Hour after hour. Day after day. You must have a cast iron ass. The picture needs that ass. I need it. *(He indicates the still-frozen Selznick —)* He needs it even more. *(Beat —)* Okay, so I'm not — you know — you and him — you're — from the same — you know — from —

BEN HECHT. Jewtown?

VIC FLEMING. I think you could walk out on me, but not on him.

BEN HECHT. Watch me.

VIC FLEMING. And you need him. Because there's only one person who'd ever make the kind of bullshit movies you want to make. *(Hecht takes a deep breath, locks the door again.)*

BEN HECHT. Okay — he gets his five days — but you're the one who's going to have to figure how to sell the slap —

VIC FLEMING. I'll find a way — *(He takes the key from Hecht and slips it back into Selznick's pocket.)*

BEN HECHT. I can't wait — *(Hecht hammers the typewriter keys.)* Prissy enters — Scarlett socks her. Action? *(Hecht pulls the sheet of paper out, thrusts it at Fleming. "Action" pulls Selznick out of his trance —)*

SELZNICK. What happened?

BEN HECHT. We lost you for a minute.

SELZNICK. *(To Hecht.)* Have we got it? The slap? Tell me we've got it.

BEN HECHT. I did my bit — *(Selznick looks at Fleming —)*

SELZNICK. So? *(Fleming holds the sheet, starts to pace —)*

VIC FLEMING. Okay, yes, right — *(He keeps pacing, looking for inspiration —)* Prissy — Scarlett — *(He stares at the sheet, as if looking for inspiration —)* Scarlett — Prissy —

SELZNICK. *(To Fleming, impatient.)* And?

VIC FLEMING. She comes up the stairs — *(Selznick sketches an imaginary sound stage —)*

SELZNICK. You've got a crew of one hundred and fifty standing around — any minute you're going to lose the light — they're all waiting for you — the tech guys, the actors — you're the one guy besides me who has to look as if he knows what he's doing —

VIC FLEMING. She comes up the stairs —

SELZNICK. You're the guy who invented the camera dolly, the traveling mike — You're going to let this little thing beat you?

BEN HECHT. *(Goading.) Toot toot —*

VIC FLEMING. Okay — *(He throws an experimental slap at Hecht.)*

BEN HECHT. Hey —

VIC FLEMING. Or maybe — *(He throws a variation of the slap.)*

SELZNICK. You don't think a — *(Selznick snakes out a slap at Fleming.)* Or a — ?

VIC FLEMING. I think a — *(He slaps Selznick.)*

BEN HECHT. It's not more of a — ? *(He slaps Fleming.)*

SELZNICK. It's more like a — *(He also slaps Fleming.)*

VIC FLEMING. We could — *(He slaps Selznick, who slaps Hecht, who slaps him back. Selznick slaps Fleming, who slaps Hecht. Hecht goes to slap Fleming, who ducks. Hecht slaps Selznick instead. A free-for-all begins, with papers and peanuts thrown all over the room as their frustrations with each other explode. In the melee Hecht tries to escape but the door to the outer office is locked again.)*

BEN HECHT. Let me out! Open the door! *(He sees Fleming bearing down on him, picks up a floor fan to defend himself with.)*

VIC FLEMING. I've got it —

SELZNICK. I don't have a scene if I don't have the slap —

VIC FLEMING. Will you listen? It's all about where I put the camera — Stick it here — *(He takes the floor fan, places it one side of*

Hecht —) Put Prissy there — *(He maneuvers Hecht into place* —)
Throw the mitt — *(He slaps the groggy Hecht again* —) Then you
get the head coming into the camera, wham, like it's come loose —
SELZNICK. Which is what I don't want —

VIC FLEMING. So we do the shot this way instead — *(He takes
the fan/camera to the other side of Hecht* —) We stick the camera
here — and pop — *(He slaps Hecht again* —) It takes the *YOW!*
off it —

SELZNICK. You think we can sell it?

VIC FLEMING. You want to see it the other way again? *(He
shapes up to the dazed Hecht again and can't resist making a fist as he
readies the blow. Hecht goes flying over the couch.)*

SELZNICK. You were right the first time — *(He snaps his fingers
at Hecht* —) Let's go. You still owe me three days.

BEN HECHT. Two.

SELZNICK. But who's counting? *(Hecht crawls back to the typewriter.)* Roll 'em — *(As Scarlett.) Where is she? Where is that bad, stupid girl?*

VIC FLEMING. Do I *have* to play Prissy?

SELZNICK. Yes.

VIC FLEMING. *Here I is, Miss Scarlett* —

SELZNICK. *The doctor — where's the doctor?*

VIC FLEMING. *I don't got no doctor* — *(Selznick pulls back his
hand to hit him* —) Wait — *(He positions the camera where he's
going to take the shot from* —) It's the angle, always the angle —
Action — *(Selznick slaps him, turns to Hecht* —)

SELZNICK. You writing, Ben? *(Hecht wearily starts to type again* —)

BEN HECHT. Heaven help us all, I am —

SELZNICK. The slap stays in the movie. The Civil War stays in
the movie. And before anybody asks — Scarlett O'Hara stays in
the movie — *(He holds the book over his head* —) Twenty-two
chapters down — forty-one to go — *(As Fleming looks for a place
to collapse again, Hecht resumes that frantic typing ...)*

End of Act One

ACT TWO

The typing becomes more and more labored as the lights come up, at dawn two days later to reveal the room in even more of a mess — apocalyptically so, in fact. Two of the chairs lie upside down, pictures hang crookedly on the walls, the bookcase doors hang open and one of the drapes has been tied into a knot. Selznick is curled in a fetal position on his desk, comatose. Hecht is typing, one letter at a time, using the last of his strength. Fleming is on his hands and knees, looking for something on the floor. He finds it. It's the one remaining banana. He clutches it to him, hiding it from the others. The intercom buzzer sounds and Selznick jerks awake —

MISS POPPENGHUL. Mr. Mayer's on the line again, Mr. Selznick —

SELZNICK. I said no calls —

MISS POPPENGHUL. Yes, Mr. Selznick —

SELZNICK. More peanuts, Miss Poppenghul —

MISS POPPENGHUL. Yes, Mr. Selznick — *(Fleming tries to peel the banana but doesn't have the strength to pull the top part open. Frustrated with trying to open it with his hands, he places it on a chair, jams it under his foot, pulls upwards. He's still too weak to split it open. Miss Poppenghul totters into the room with another bowl of peanuts. Her hair is disordered, her dress crumpled, her voice is shaky, sounds a little odd, as if this normally superhumanly efficient woman is also suffering from the ordeal —)* Will you speak to Miss Leigh, Mr. Selznick? She sounds awfully upset —

SELZNICK. Okay — *(He fumbles for a phone, listens —)* Yes … I know … I understand that … but I have every confidence in Victor Fleming — *(He looks towards Fleming, who is staring brokenly at the banana he can't peel — Listens.)* What thing with Garland — ? *(Listens.)* I never heard about a slap — *(Listens.)* Come Monday, I think you're going to be very happy with him and the new screenplay — *(Hecht snores. Hecht's almost up to the last scene — He aims a banana skin at Hecht, who has momentarily stopped typing as his head slumps on the typewriter in sleep. Hecht wakes as Selznick puts the phone down, presses the buzzer* —)

MISS POPPENGHUL. Yes, Mr. Selznick? *(He jumps, swings wildly around at her, stares at her, recovers.)*

SELZNICK. Memo to — *(He shakes his head, trying to think of somebody to send a memo to* —)

MISS POPPENGHUL. Memo to, Mr. Selznick — ?

SELZNICK. Memo to — memo to — well send everybody a memo — about everything — *(As Miss Poppenghul wearily exits, Fleming looks wildly around the room* —)

VIC FLEMING. The Chinaman —

BEN HECHT. The Chinaman?

VIC FLEMING. The one-legged Chinaman who was dancing on the piano — ? With the redhead in the barrel? Over there, with all the fish — *(He looks over his head, as if trying to see something* —) Up there —

SELZNICK. Don't *you* lose it now — *(Fleming peels away from him, heads to the window, opens a blind and peers through* —)

VIC FLEMING. The cops. Somebody's got to have missed me. They'll have the place staked out. You think you can get away with this?

SELZNICK. Ben — where are we up to?

BEN HECHT. Bonnie just died — I think — I know *somebody* fell off a horse —

SELZNICK. *(To Fleming.)* You see how near we are to getting out of here? *(Fleming pulls the blind up* —)

VIC FLEMING. Don't shoot! *(Fleming puts his hands in the air.)*

SELZNICK. Get away from the window. *(Fleming lets the blind drop again, his shoulders sag* —)

VIC FLEMING. This is what the Lindbergh kid must have gone through, poor little bastard.

SELZNICK. Victor! *(Fleming shudders as he looks around the room* —)

VIC FLEMING. Oh God, it's real, then.

SELZNICK. Eat your banana —

VIC FLEMING. I only have one kidney, you know that?

SELZNICK. Don't tell me you can't take the heat?

VIC FLEMING. Who could take this?

SELZNICK. *(Encouraging.)* What about that shot you had in *Test Pilot*? When you had a hundred and ten planes in the air at one time — ? Eighteen cameras — ?

VIC FLEMING. That was easier than this — *(He chews on the*

banana as he totters to the couch —) Why are you doing this to us? What are you trying to prove? If it's because your dad went overnight from a mansion on Park Avenue to a one-room apartment — ? Because a Mayer's always had you by the balls — ? whether it was Louis or Irene —

SELZNICK. I don't need counselling from a Cherokee German.

VIC FLEMING. You know what the odds are against this movie, even if you don't kill Hecht before he's done?

SELZNICK. I'll remind you you said that — when you pick up your Oscar.

VIC FLEMING. So *that's* why we're being put through this? *(He cradles an imaginary Oscar —)*

SELZNICK. Feel pretty good, wouldn't it — having that little fella on your desk?

VIC FLEMING. I always thought they made it look like a big gold pecker. Probably not by accident. *(Selznick hears Hecht falter —)*

SELZNICK. Keep at it, Ben —

VIC FLEMING. You want to win so you can piss on Mayer on the way up to collect it.

SELZNICK. I want to win because the movies are dead. It's over. This industry's finished. Before we turn the lights off, I want to make one great movie, to show just how good it could have been.

VIC FLEMING. *(Protesting.)* Our careers may be over after this but Hollywood's never been in better shape —

SELZNICK. Hollywood? The town had thirty great years. Amazing years. Who could have imagined when it all began that some of the biggest fortunes on the planet were going to be made by making people sit in a room full of strangers, many of them probably tubercular, switching the lights off and throwing pictures on a glorified horse blanket? But we didn't just kill the goose that laid the golden egg — we stuck the golden egg up its ass and fricasseed it.

VIC FLEMING. Hollywood's going to make over three hundred movies this year.

SELZNICK. Tell me how in the name of God that can't be three hundred variations of the same dumb story and the same dumb bunch of characters. *(He pulls a large drawer open. It contains movie posters. He pulls them out, holds them up before dropping them to the floor at his feet, taking out another —)* The girl next door, the hooker with a heart of gold, the broad, the flirt, the tease. The good guy, the bad guy, the funny guy, the sidekick, the fresh kid — *(His shoulders go down —)* In a few years this place is going to be like

Egypt. Full of crumbling pyramids. And when it's all over, what have the movies been? A flood of claptrap that's helped bitch up the world. Thirty years and maybe one good movie.

VIC FLEMING. *Test Pilot? (He hears Hecht falter again —)*

SELZNICK. But I need the screenplay. Ben, come on — I know these aren't the ideal conditions to work in — *(Hecht reacts, almost at the end of his tether —)*

BEN HECHT. Believe me, the loneliness of literary creation is seldom part of movie writing — not with the phone ringing like a firehouse bell, the boss charging in and out of your atelier, the director tearing his hair out, waiting for the pages. *More peanuts, Miss Poppenghul?* Ideal? *(Selznick appeals to him again —)*

SELZNICK. But for me, Ben? Please? The last reel — ?

VIC FLEMING. Melanie's on the couch, about to croak —

SELZNICK. In the biggest damn tear-jerker of a scene that's ever been put on film — *(Hecht rounds on Selznick, his tormentor —)*

BEN HECHT. Why don't you ask yourself why you always prefer the classics. Costume drama. Dead books by dead writers. Now you have a book that could be made to mean something, you're still trying to play it safe —

SELZNICK. Me? Play it safe? I'm the biggest gambler in Hollywood.

BEN HECHT. A handful of Jews gave the world the movies but deep down you're scared we'll be run out of town, one day — all us Mayers and Goldwyns and Zukors and Cohns and Hechts — we'll be chased back to Russia or Poland or Hungary, back to the *stetls,* where we'll be glove salesmen, furriers, pants pressers again — we'll have lost it all — the cars, the houses, the blonde *shiksas.*

VIC FLEMING. The hell with it. I just want to get the goddamn screenplay finished. My grandfather actually fought in the Civil War. *(Hecht rounds on him —)*

BEN HECHT. So?

VIC FLEMING. So the last reel —

BEN HECHT. *(Persisting.)* Somehow that makes you more American than us? *(To Selznick.)* You hear that? *(Fleming looks like he's about to explode with the effort of containing his frustration —)*

VIC FLEMING. Uh. *Uh. Uhhhhhhh!*

SELZNICK. I don't think he's saying that. *(Hecht won't let it go —)*

BEN HECHT. So what are you saying? What do you think about being locked in a room with two crazy Jews, Victor? Really?

VIC FLEMING. It wouldn't be the first time.

BEN HECHT. Not in Hollywood, that's for sure — right, *Victor?*

VIC FLEMING. Well that would be a fact, wouldn't it? *(Selznick pulls Hecht away from Fleming —)*

SELZNICK. What are you trying to do? Make him walk out of here? Sabotage the movie? *(Hecht breaks free of Selznick —)*

BEN HECHT. I'm looking at a place in Beverly Hills right now. Who was Beverly? The wife of the developer. He built it because Jews can't live in Hancock Park — *(Angled to Selznick.)* No matter how much money they have, how many movies they make.

VIC FLEMING. Yeah, well, the movie we're trying to make right now is *Gone with the Wind* — *(Hecht turns to Selznick —)*

BEN HECHT. You may be a prince of Hollywood, David, but you know you can't you any country club in Los Angeles you want or live any place you like. Admit it.

SELZNICK. Why don't you keep your politics, obsessions, bees in your bonnet and personal opinions out of my studio?

BEN HECHT. Isn't that exactly where they should be? Where yours should be? You remember Plato's cave?

VIC FLEMING. *(Sneering.)* Isn't that a roadhouse in Topanga?

SELZNICK. Plato!

BEN HECHT. Plato says we're like men staring at the wall, seeing flickering shadows from the fire behind us, trying to figure what they mean. What's that but a movie theater? Forget these goddamn melodramas and make something about real people for a change, living real lives.

VIC FLEMING. People go to the movies because real life stinks. They want to see something *larger* than life up there.

BEN HECHT. *(Persisting, to Selznick.)* Why don't you take a real gamble and make a movie that could make America look its ugly face in the mirror?

SELZNICK. Because that's not what it wants to see. It wants to see the way it *thinks* it looks.

BEN HECHT. And that's okay by you?

SELZNICK. And you? You've done pretty good for yourself out here. Ever walk away from a paycheck? *(Hecht's momentarily off balance —)*

BEN HECHT. I take the money and run and keep coming back for more, yes — thank you for pointing that out — *(Hecht sinks into his chair with the despair of exhaustion —)* Maybe they just put the American movie industry in the wrong place. Out here in the desert. With that sun frying your brains. Where it's always, like, two-thirty on a Tuesday afternoon. Where when you listen hard enough you can hear your brain cells tinkling as they hit the ground. Who could do any real work here? Maybe only the Jews would be crazy enough or broke enough to try to build something here. Or maybe we see something that reminds us of home. The Mohave — the Negev? Are they so different? It's just hard to accept that the guy with the whip is always another Jew —

SELZNICK. We're back to Hitler? Mussolini?

VIC FLEMING. We should be back to Melanie —

SELZNICK. At least Fleming is honest. He doesn't give a shit —

VIC FLEMING. *(Flattered.)* That's right.

SELZNICK. Nobody's got a gun to your head. You could walk out of here right now —

BEN HECHT. I said I'd give you five days.

SELZNICK. So get your ass in that chair — *(He turns to Fleming —)* Yes, my grandfather was probably behind a pushcart somewhere in Russia when yours was fighting the Civil War. *(He grabs the tattered novel —)* But I'm the one making our *War and Peace* —

BEN HECHT. *Our War and Peace? (Selznick whipsaws back to Hecht —)*

SELZNICK. You want to see everything through a six-pointed star, go right ahead. That's your problem, not mine. Nobody's going to send us anyplace — we're *Americans* now.

BEN HECHT. Is that right, David? Give me twenty seconds — *(He presses the intercom button —)* Is Nunnally Johnson on the lot?

MISS POPPENGHUL. Yes, Mr. Hecht —

BEN HECHT. Get him for me, please —

MISS POPPENGHUL. Right away, Mr. Hecht.

SELZNICK. What are you doing?

BEN HECHT. Wait and see — *(A ring tone sounds from the intercom —)*

NUNNALLY JOHNSON'S VOICE. Nunnally Johnson here —

BEN HECHT. It's Ben. I have a question for you. David Selznick — is he an American or a Jew?

NUNNALLY JOHNSON'S VOICE. He's a Jew.

BEN HECHT. I'll be in touch. *(He thumbs the intercom off.)*

SELZNICK. Another pissed-off screenwriter? That doesn't prove anything. *(Hecht thumbs the intercom again —)*

BEN HECHT. Get me Martin Quigley.

SELZNICK. What does it prove? *(A ring tone sounds on the intercom —)*

QUIGLEY'S VOICE. Quigley.

BEN HECHT. Hecht here. I'll make it quick. David O. Selznick

— Jew or American?

QUIGLEY'S VOICE. How can he be an American? Even the O's fake. He doesn't have a middle name.

BEN HECHT. Thank you. *(He thumbs the intercom off.)*

SELZNICK. It's a setup. He was always too pally with Thalberg.

BEN HECHT. You tell me who to phone.

SELZNICK. We don't have time for this.

BEN HECHT. Are you scared to find out?

SELZNICK. Your agent.

BEN HECHT. Okay — *(He thumbs the intercom —)* Get me Leland Hayward —

SELZNICK. Then we finish the scenario — *(Another ring tone sounds —)*

HAYWARD'S VOICE. Hayward. Who's that?

BEN HECHT. It's Ben Hecht. Settle a bet for me. David O. Selznick is on the *Titanic*. There are two lifeboats. One filled with Jews, one with Americans. Which one would you put him in?

HAYWARD'S VOICE. He goes down with the Jews.

BEN HECHT. That's all I wanted to know. *(He looks towards Selznick, who's digesting the betrayals.)* You can make their *War and Peace* for them. You're still going to be a *Selznick. (It takes a moment for Selznick to recover from the blow of the phone calls. He takes a deep breath.)*

SELZNICK. So you've just proved how clever a guy you are, Ben. Me — I never even finished college. I had to do my growing up on a movie lot. All I've known is the sound stage and the commissary. I even married the boss' daughter. That's how limited my horizons are.

BEN HECHT. You're one of the smartest men I ever met.

SELZNICK. But I'm not a Man of Ideas, like you. I'm too busy making movies.

BEN HECHT. That's not all there is to the world —

SELZNICK. I like to think I have some ideas, too, but I'm not a writer. I can't put them on the page, make a parade of them. But movies don't get made by Men of Ideas. Nothing happens anywhere without the Men of Action — *(Fleming jerks awake —)*

VIC FLEMING. *(Automatic.)* Action —

BEN HECHT. The guys with the power? — As who else might say, wearing a little black moustache and lederhosen?

SELZNICK. What power do I have, Ben? I can't make you finish the screenplay, I can't make people go see my movies, I can't fix the rocks in those guys' heads and I'm not about to waste my time trying. You want to talk about power? You know who has the power in the end? The real power?

VIC FLEMING. Mayer —

SELZNICK. No.

BEN HECHT. The Hays Office —

SELZNICK. Not even close.

VIC FLEMING. The banks —

SELZNICK. No — *(Selznick points to the photo of the crowd outside Grauman's Chinese Theater on his wall again. He jabs a thumb at an anonymous face in the crowd —)* This guy here — *(Jabs it at another face —)* Her — *(Another one —)* I have to keep this guy happy — *(Another one —)* This one — *(Another one —)* This son of a bitch here — *(Another one —)* This jerk — *(Another one —)* That asshole — *(Another one —)* Fatso, here — *(Another one —)* Baldy — *(Another one —)* The gimp — *(Another one —)* Her with the big tits — *(Another one —)* Him with the boil on his nose — *(More faces —)* This Irishman, that Polak, Giovanni, Mike, Hans, Mr. and Mrs. Wong, the Dutchman, the wop — *(Even more —)* The farmer, the shopgirl, the clerk, the housewife, the masseuse, the factory hand, the short-order cook — *(Even more —)* All those Joe Blows and Jane Does, the guy with the lunch pail, the broad in the elevator, all those little people who have nothing in common except they go to the movies three or four times a week and every time they go they buy a ticket and every ticket is a vote for my movie or a vote against it. They're the people who hand out the ulcers, pal, they're the ones who run this town, the world, they have the power, the real power. Mayer? Me? Hedda Hopper? Gable? We don't amount to anything if they give us the thumbs-down. Princes of Hollywood? America's royalty? We are down on our knees sucking the collective dick of the Great Unwashed.

BEN HECHT. That's democracy.

SELZNICK. And brother, do I hate it. Because to stay in business you have to give them what they want, not what's good for them.

VIC FLEMING. You can't blame how lousy the movies are on the movie audience — cretins though most of them are —

SELZNICK. They bought the book. I hope they go see the movie. That's all I can do. But I'll make it my way, in my studio. If they like it I'll be the Boy Wonder again. If they don't —

VIC FLEMING. It's all a crap shoot, anyway. You bust your balls on something that's a surefire hit, it makes three hundred bucks and lies there like a yak turd. Or on the other hand you take garbage like this —

SELZNICK. That's very encouraging, Victor. *(Trying to rally them for one final effort —)* Ask yourself why we do this, fellas. Why we put ourselves through it. Why a guy like you risks losing your eye for a picture?

VIC FLEMING. *(Hand to his eye.)* Don't say that —

BEN HECHT. The money?

SELZNICK. There's easier ways to make a living. But people who make railroad switchgear don't get up every morning feeling like we do. Soap manufacturers don't. Real estate brokers don't. The whole world wants to work in the movies. Not just because of the money or because of the glamour of that out there —

BEN HECHT. The studio? That stockyard for the human soul?

SELZNICK. It's only in the movies where the dead can walk. You have any other way to live forever?

VIC FLEMING. *(Taking charge.)* The last reel — *(Hecht totters back to the typewriter, Fleming heads thankfully to the couch —)*

SELZNICK. We've got them on the edge of their seats. For three hours they've lived with Scarlett and Rhett and Ashley and Melanie, they've fought and suffered alongside them. A million eyes are fixed on the screen, a million hearts are beating in tune with our characters — *(Fleming lies on the couch as Melanie, dying —)*

VIC FLEMING. Melanie's on the couch, about to cash in her chips —

SELZNICK. *(At Hecht.)* Here's the sockeroo. Wait 'til you get a load of this — *(Selznick kneels alongside Fleming, holds his hand —)* Before Melanie dies she tells Scarlett —

VIC FLEMING. *Be good to Rhett — he really loves you — aaaaaaaah* — *(He twists feverishly, miming Melanie's death, then arches his back, twitches and dies.)*

SELZNICK. Scarlett's now free to marry Ashley but she finds out that the big milksop never really loved her, not like he loved Melanie — *(Throwing himself into Scarlett again, running his hands over his body —)* It was this you wanted, this — *(As Ashley —)* I guess it was, Scarlett — *(As Scarlett —)* I've been a silly little fool. It's Rhett I really love — She rushes back to Rhett — running, running, running — *(As Scarlett, running around the office —)* I've been blind and stupid all these years, that's what I've been, it's always been Rhett — Rhett — Rhett — *(Hecht is typing grimly —)*

BEN HECHT. *Rhett — Rhett — Rhett —*

SELZNICK. But he's staring at her with a cold glint in his eye, as if he's never seen her before — *(As Scarlett, recoiling.) Don't look at me like that* — *(He puts his hand to his heart, backs away as Fleming sneers* — *)*

VIC FLEMING. *Melanie was worth a million of you* —

SELZNICK. *I know that now* —

VIC FLEMING. *I expect you'll be shacking up with ole Ashley now* —

SELZNICK. *No, no, it's you I love* — *Rhett* — *Rhett* — *(To Hecht.)* Are you getting this, Ben?

BEN HECHT. Am I ever — *(Selznick holds his arms out for an embrace but Fleming/Rhett moves away* — *)*

VIC FLEMING. *And I loved you, kid* —

SELZNICK. *Loved* — ?

VIC FLEMING. *But you screwed it up. Time and again. You couldn't get that damn wishy-washy Ashley out of your head. And now it's too late* —

SELZNICK. *Too late* — ? *(Fleming heads to the door* — *)*

VIC FLEMING. *It's goodbye, Toots* — *forever* —

SELZNICK. *No* — *(He throws himself on the floor, grabs Fleming's ankle* — *)*

VIC FLEMING. *You're easy on the eye and a hellcat in the sack* — *but it's time to blow* — *(He opens the door* — *)*

SELZNICK. *Rhett* —

VIC FLEMING. *Can it, sister* — *(He shakes his ankle free* — *) It's the big fade-out.*

SELZNICK. *What about me?*

VIC FLEMING. *My dear, I don't give a shit* —

SELZNICK. *Damn,* he doesn't give a *damn.*

BEN HECHT. You can't use that line. *(Selznick grimaces* — *)*

SELZNICK. Ben's right.

BEN HECHT. You'll never get "damn" past the Hays Office.

SELZNICK. That's not the problem. *(To Fleming* — *)* Say it again.

VIC FLEMING. *My dear, I don't give a damn.*

SELZNICK. Again.

VIC FLEMING. *My dear, I don't give a damn.*

SELZNICK. There's something wrong — *(He screws his face up, tasting the words as he speaks them* — *) I don't give a* — *I don't give a* — *(Frustrated* — *)* It needs a handle —

VIC FLEMING. Does it matter?

SELZNICK. They showed me the one-sheet for that gorilla movie I made. I said you can't call it *Kong. King Kong. That's* a handle —

VIC FLEMING. Just let him finish the goddamn screenplay —

(Hecht impatiently hammers the keys —)

BEN HECHT. Melanie dies, Scarlett gets the brushoff from Rhett and then — ?

SELZNICK. He walks out.

BEN HECHT. And?

VIC FLEMING. That's the end of the book.

BEN HECHT. Wait wait wait — *(Blearily he rubs his eyes, grabs the book, turns to the last page —)* The end?

SELZNICK. *Finis. (The bewildered Hecht is flipping the page backwards and forwards —)*

BEN HECHT. What did I miss? Did we drop some scenes? Do they end up together or don't they?

SELZNICK. Yes.

BEN HECHT. What do you mean, yes?

SELZNICK. No.

BEN HECHT. Yes or no?

SELZNICK. Yes *and* no.

BEN HECHT. *And* no?

SELZNICK. No.

BEN HECHT. No?

SELZNICK. Yes.

BEN HECHT. *Do they or don't they?*

VIC FLEMING. Is it important?

BEN HECHT. I've been hanging on five days to find out —

SELZNICK. It's how Margaret Mitchell ends the book —

BEN HECHT. Wait — *(He grabs the cover, which is hanging by a thread —)* This is Book One, right? There's another volume?

VIC FLEMING. *(Shudders.)* Don't even suggest it —

BEN HECHT. After all that Rhett walks out? With nothing decided? We don't know whether she gets him back, whether he changes his mind — ? Whether he gets run over by the fire wagon the moment he steps off the sidewalk — ? You can't end a movie like that.

SELZNICK. It's how the book ends and a million and a half people bought the book.

BEN HECHT. So a million and a half people threw it at the dog when they got to the last page?

SELZNICK. We can't rewrite the ending. It wouldn't be *Gone with the Wind.*

BEN HECHT. This from the man who let W.C. Fields throw a juggling routine into *David Copperfield*?

SELZNICK. When you buy a book you buy what the writer got

51

wrong as well as what they got right.

BEN HECHT. So you *know* this ending doesn't work?

SELZNICK. I also know not to mess with it — *(Hecht turns to Fleming —)*

BEN HECHT. Do you think you can end a movie like that?

VIC FLEMING. I don't care any more. I just want to get out of here and onto the set. *(Brokenly.)* I want to feel the wind on my face, hear the cries of children at play, have a little puppy lick my hand. Finish it any damn way you please — just finish it —

SELZNICK. I can't change Margaret Mitchell's ending.

BEN HECHT. But you know it doesn't work?

VIC FLEMING. *(Wavering.)* I'll shoot any ending you want, David, but this one is a little —

BEN HECHT. It's not an ending. It's like she said, "The hell with this, let *them* figure it out, I'm going to worm the parakeet — "

SELZNICK. It's got its problems but I'm not going to change it —

BEN HECHT. The last card always reads *The End*. Not — *Kind of the End.*

VIC FLEMING. You wouldn't shoot a little — *an alternative ending?*

BEN HECHT. Or *The Best Ending We Can Think of Right Now but If We Can Think of a Better One We'll Get Back to You —*

VIC FLEMING. A little insurance? If it doesn't preview well? *(Fleming indicates the typewriter —)* You don't mind if I — ?

BEN HECHT. Go right ahead — *(Fleming sits, starts to type —)*

VIC FLEMING. We keep the same dialogue B.S. but we cut to Scarlett looking up —

BEN HECHT. One of these? *(Hecht mimes Scarlett.)*

VIC FLEMING. Then we hear galloping hoofbeats and Rhett rides back, he scoops her up, in his arms —

BEN HECHT. He leaps a fence —

VIC FLEMING. He jumps a ditch —

BEN HECHT. A wild glint in his eye —

VIC FLEMING. A cruel smile on his lips —

BEN HECHT. They ride off together, her hair streaming in the wind —

VIC FLEMING. I love the hair —

BEN HECHT. He says —

VIC FLEMING. *You silly little fool —*

BEN HECHT. And she sighs —

VIC FLEMING. *Oh, Rhett —*

BEN HECHT. They jump another fence —

VIC FLEMING. And gallop into the sunset —

BEN HECHT. *That's* how to end a movie — *(Fleming, flushed with the pride of authorship, pulls the sheet of paper out of the type-writer and hands it to Selznick. He's tempted —)*

SELZNICK. That's — that's how to end a movie. But it's not how she ends the book. Because she knows. She *knows,* too. *(Regretfully he crumples the paper up and drops it on the floor with the other detritus —)* Ben — *(He snaps his fingers and Fleming moves away from the typewriter. Selznick hands Hecht the book, opened to the last page —)* Bring it home. *(Hecht reads —)*

BEN HECHT. Tomorrow is — *(Anguished, disbelieving.)* No no no no no no. Is that the last line? Isn't it obvious that *tomorrow's another day?*

VIC FLEMING. Ben, please —

BEN HECHT. It's a hell of a long wait to be told that.

SELZNICK. Put the button on it. *(Hecht writhes in agony, as if every fiber of his writer's soul is rebelling at writing those words —)*

BEN HECHT. Ah — ah — ah — *(Fleming goes behind Hecht, massages his shoulders, kneading them like a boxer's second —)*

VIC FLEMING. You can do it, Ben. Sure you can. *(He grabs a glass of water, makes Hecht drink, then pats him on the back so that he spits the water into a vase —)* Attaboy — *(He kneads Hecht's fingers —)* One more line —

BEN HECHT. I can't — *(His hands are shaking, he's genuinely unable to write another line — especially not that line.)* Not that line, no — don't make me — *(He makes a run towards the door.)*

VIC FLEMING. We lost him —

SELZNICK. Come back, Ben, come back —

VIC FLEMING. It's no good — *(Hecht has reached the door. He's about to open it when Selznick bursts into song —)*

SELZNICK. *Da da da da — (Taken by surprise, Hecht is stalled for a moment.)* I know what I do to make sense of the world — or if not make sense of it, keep too busy to be scared there is no sense. I make movies. *(He sees Hecht is about to bolt —) Da da da — V*ic finds his way to make some kind of order every day, out of the chaos of a movie set. You mold a shapeless world with the power of words. Sure, these aren't yours and who the hell knows what they mean — *(He indicates the desk —)* But you don't have a choice — it's what you do. *(Hecht groans and brokenly types the last few words of the screenplay. As he does so Selznick heads to the intercom —)* Do I have any other meetings today?

MISS POPPENGHUL. Thirty-two, Mr. Selznick. And Security wants to know what to do about the writer you had arrested.

SELZNICK. Okay. Come in here and clean this place up, would you? And then bring me some breakfast.

MISS POPPENGHUL. Mr. Mayer is still holding —

SELZNICK. Twenty seconds — *(To Hecht.)* How are we doing, Ben? *(He snaps his fingers, impatiently —)* You think this is the only movie I have in development? I've got *Intermezzo* and *Rebecca* to worry about.

BEN HECHT. *(Typing.)* Tomorrow is — I need hardly say — another — but Selznick seems to think it needs saying — another day. *(He slumps in his seat, exhausted, nauseated by the writing of the last line as Miss Poppenghul enters. She moves in an uncoordinated, dazed way as she picks up scripts, rearranges the furniture, puts right all the disorder.)* Fade out. Roll end titles.

VIC FLEMING. The end?

BEN HECHT. — of our careers, yes.

VIC FLEMING. Really the end?

BEN HECHT. Good night, Vienna — *(Even Selznick looks as if he's having trouble believing it —)*

SELZNICK. We did it?

BEN HECHT. I guess we did — *(He takes the last page out, stares at it in wonder —)* My God — we did. *(Brokenly he gets to his feet, tries to unbend his fingers, straighten out his back as Selznick grabs the screenplay, starts flicking through it —)*

SELZNICK. One. Exterior. Day. Tara. Field hands labor under a blood-red sky — *(The lights isolate him as he intently reads, his creation coming to life on the soundtrack as we hear drumbeats getting nearer and near —)* Scarlett … Melanie … Ashley … Rhett … *(Now we hear "Dixie" in the far distance —)* Good … good … not bad … good — *("Dixie" is countered by "The Battle Hymn of the Republic" as he skims the pages, the sheets flying through his fingers.)* Ah — The North attacks — *(Battle is joined on the soundtrack; he sways as cannons boom, muskets crackle, men cry out —)* The slap — *(We hear the sound of Prissy being slapped followed by a baby cry —)* Atlanta burns — *(We hear the crackling of flames —)* Back to Tara — *(We hear the sound of a horse-drawn wagon, the crack of a whip —)* She shoots the — *(We hear a gunshot —)* Never be hungry — *(We hear someone take a bite out of a carrot —)* The lumberyard — *(We hear the buzz of a sawmill —)* She marries Rhett — *(We hear dance music —)* Bonnie jumps the — *(We hear galloping hoofbeats, a horse's neigh and a sharp crack as Bonnie hits the deck* — *)* Ashley Melanie Scarlett Rhett — Ashley Scarlett — Scarlett Melanie — Scarlett Ashley — Scarlett Rhett — Scarlett — Scarlett — Scarlett — Scarlett — *(We hear church bells sound* — *)* Tomorrow, I'll think of some way to get him back. After all, tomorrow is … *(Miss Poppenghul gives a heartfelt sigh but Hecht isn't impressed* — *)*

BEN HECHT. A terrible line to end a movie on. *(Fleming can see the shot, frames it with his fingers as he and Selznick head upstage* — *)*

VIC FLEMING. And I put the camera here — maybe an eighteen — and I go in close and then I pull back and — *(They turn to face the window. As they do so Miss Poppenghul has coincidentally reached its center, behind Selznick's desk. In her red dress she's holding up one of the bananas she's been collecting. She looks oddly like Scarlett in her iconic "never be hungry again" pose …* *)*

SELZNICK. It's perfect, Ben — *(The lights change, the Poppenghul/Scarlett illusion goes. Selznick's throat works, his voice is hoarse with emotion* — *)* I don't want to change a line.

BEN HECHT. I'm off assignment?

SELZNICK. It's a work of genius.

BEN HECHT. I can go?

SELZNICK. Sure. There's nothing we can't fix later. *(There's a moment when it looks as if all his strength has gone. Then he pulls himself upright and through the next speeches changes into clean shirt, new tie and fresh suit. To Miss Poppenghul.)* Typists. Get me typists. Lots of typists. Memo to all departments. Art — camera — grips — electrics — wardrobe — props — transport — marketing — publicity — stills — catering — finance — stenographers — continuity — extras casting — the script is locked. We start shooting first thing Monday. Actors on the set in make-up and costume at six A.M.

MISS POPPENGHUL. Yes Mr. Selznick — *(Selznick catches the exhausted Fleming mid-yawn* — *)*

SELZNICK. What are you waiting for? *(He pushes the screenplay into his hands* — *)* We need a shot list and call sheet by tonight.

VIC FLEMING. Shot list — call sheet —

SELZNICK. *(To Hecht.)* Are you still here?

BEN HECHT. My check? *(Fleming is heading wearily to the door* — *)*

VIC FLEMING. Shot list … call sheet —

SELZNICK. Keep on top of Vivien Leigh's cleavage. If she's playing a tramp she's got to look like one. And no cubed ice, okay? You'll have that shot list on my desk by six?

VIC FLEMING. I'm going to be allowed to finish this movie?

SELZNICK. Sure. And you can take a fee up front or I'll give you a piece of the gross. What do you say?

VIC FLEMING. Thanks but I know a turkey when I see one. I'll take the fee.

SELZNICK. But you're ready to do this, right? Now that we have a script?

VIC FLEMING. David, you and I know the screenplay's just the pimple on the ass of the production.

BEN HECHT. Oh, really?

VIC FLEMING. Now the man's work starts — *(Fleming squares his shoulders, readying himself for the immense task ahead. As he heads to the door with the script he gives Hecht a look of grudging admiration —)* But you did pretty good, at that.

BEN HECHT. Good luck. You're going to need it. *(Fleming hesitates —)*

VIC FLEMING. What did you really think of *Test Pilot*?

BEN HECHT. I don't think you could make a better movie. *(Fleming decides to take it as a compliment, exits as Miss Poppenghul exits with the cart.)*

SELZNICK. *(To Hecht.)* Fifteen thousand dollars? *(Hecht watches as Selznick writes one check —)* What's the name of that movie I pulled Fleming off?

BEN HECHT. *The Wizard of Oz.*

SELZNICK. There's a character in it, right, the guy everybody's scared of — ?

BEN HECHT. The Wizard of Oz —

SELZNICK. I know the title — the name of the character?

BEN HECHT. The Wizard of Oz.

SELZNICK. No, there's a character who turns out to be just this guy sitting behind a curtain, pulling levers and making funny voices and stuff so everybody's scared of him? But he's just a guy, right? Not a monster. Not a Hitler or a Stalin or a Mussolini. Just a guy. *(He tears out the check.)* What do I have, Ben? What does Sam Goldwyn have? What — okay — did Thalberg have? What's a producer, when you get down to it? Just a guy with a phone and a desk and a fly buzzing in his ear with an idea for a movie and willing to ride his hunch. *(He hands Hecht the check.)*

BEN HECHT. You know what a gamble this particular movie is?

SELZNICK. The movies are the biggest gamble there is and Hollywood's rigged the game — but it's the only game in town.

BEN HECHT. But you're a born gambler and born gamblers

don't play to win. They play to lose.

SELZNICK. Is that right?

BEN HECHT. They have to leave the table broke. Dostoyevsky used to ejaculate when he lost.

SELZNICK. I'll make a note not to sit facing him. *(He takes a deep satisfied breath, totally at peace with himself, ready to lose it all as he writes a second check.)* I'm going to roll the dice. Either I break the bank or I go belly up. My poppa might have died broke but he didn't die poor. He said, *"Always* be broke, throw it around, give it away. Living beyond your means gives a man confidence." For once I'm making a movie without any compromises — I'm going to show everybody how it should be done — and if it takes a crazy Jew to do it, what the hell, somebody else can figure out what that means — frankly, I don't give a damn — *(He hesitates —)* That's it, that's the handle. *Frankly, my dear, I don't give a damn —*

BEN HECHT. That's good —

SELZNICK. You like it?

BEN HECHT. It did need a handle. But I thought we weren't changing any of Margaret Mitchell's lines?

SELZNICK. Yeah, well, I'm the producer.

BEN HECHT. You want me to — *(He takes out a pencil, ready to make the correction.)*

SELZNICK. I'll do it. There's a couple of other things I want to noodle at — *(Miss Poppenghul enters with the breakfast cart —)*

MISS POPPENGHUL. Your breakfast, Mr. Selznick — *(Selznick writes a second check.)*

SELZNICK. What was the name of that organization you're always bugging me about? The one that helps get people out of Europe?

BEN HECHT. Jewish Relief.

SELZNICK. Jewish Relief … *(Miss Poppenghul exits as he tears the check out of the book, holds it out to Hecht, who reaches for it. Selznick doesn't let go.)* Who'd you be in the movie? Rhett? Or Ashley? What do you think? You'd be the guy looking ahead or the guy looking back?

BEN HECHT. I couldn't say — but I think you make a wonderful Scarlett O'Hara.

SELZNICK. Is there anything wrong with getting the job done, no matter what it takes?

BEN HECHT. Not if you make sure you remember who you are and what you should do about it.

SELZNICK. I gave you the check, didn't I?

BEN HECHT. Not yet. *(A momentary hesitation, then Selznick lets go of the check, grabs a pastry, heads to his desk, piled high with files, letters and scripts for other movies.)*

SELZNICK. Not so fast. I'm having a little scenario problem with *Intermezzo*. It wouldn't take much to punch it up. Are you free — *(Checks his watch.)* Say this afternoon — ?

BEN HECHT. *(Shaken.)* Am I free this afternoon? Am I — ? No. I'm just about to check myself into a mental home. Don't — just don't — don't call me, okay?

SELZNICK. Ben, I ever get myself in a hole like this again, you're the only guy I'm going to call.

BEN HECHT. Yeah ... well ... *(He covers his reaction by taking the pastry from Selznick's hand —)* I still say no Civil War movie ever made a dime. *(Hecht exits with the pastry as Miss Poppenghul enters —)*

MISS POPPENGHUL. Your coffee, Mr. Selznick.

SELZNICK. Where's my first meeting?

MISS POPPENGHUL. Coming right in, Mr. Selznick. Mr. Mayer is still on the line.

SELZNICK. Put him through, would you, Miss Poppenghul?

MISS POPPENGHUL. Yes, Mr. Selznick. *(Instinctively she reaches for her memo pad —)* Memo to who, Mr, Selznick? *(Her hand twitches as it hovers over the pad —)* Coming right in, Mr. Selznick. More peanuts, Mr. Selznick? Memo to — ? Memo to?

SELZNICK. Take the rest of the day off, Miss Poppenghul.

MISS POPPENGHUL. *(With relief.)* Thank you, Mr. Selznick —

SELZNICK. But first put Mayer through.

MISS POPPENGHUL. Yes, Mr. Selznick. Oh thank you, Mr. Selznick — *(As she exits he opens his desk drawer, takes out a pipe, sighs with anticipation, lights it, draws, savors the taste, exhales. The phone rings. He ignores it, takes the tattered remains of the book of* Gone with the Wind *and places it onto the top shelf of the bookcase. He slaps it in place, sits at the desk, takes his time answering the ringing phone, feet on the desk —)*

SELZNICK. Louis? *(Beat.) Poppa —* I have some very good news for you — *(He blows out more pipe smoke.)* We're making a movie ... *(Dawn light floods the room, echoing the red sky over Tara. Through the window we see dark figures silhouetted against a sunset and hear the overture to* Gone with the Wind *as huge marquee letters spelling out* Gone with the Wind *glimmer and sparkle and we ...)*

End of Play

PROPERTY LIST

Breakfast cart
Gone with the Wind book (SELZNICK)
Stack of papers (SELZNICK)
Legal pad and pencil (SELZNICK)
Books, magazines, scripts (SELZNICK)
Memo pad, pen (MISS POPPENGHUL)
Cart with typewriter, office supplies, ice water and glasses,
    bananas and peanuts (MISS POPPENGHUL)
Bowl of peanuts (MISS POPPENGHUL)
Script pages (HECHT)
Key (SELZNICK)
Floor fan (FLEMING)
Movie posters (SELZNICK)
Clean shirt, tie, suit (SELZNICK)
Checkbook, pen (SELZNICK)
Pipe, match (SELZNICK)

SOUND EFFECTS

Intercom buzzer
Typewriter keys
Drumbeats
"Dixie"
"Battle Hymn of the Republic"
Sounds of battle
Slap
Baby crying
Flames
Wagon
Whip
Bite of food
Sawmill
Dance music
Hoofbeats, neigh, thud
Church bell
Phone ringing
Overture to *Gone with the Wind*

NEW PLAYS

★ **THE EXONERATED by Jessica Blank and Erik Jensen.** Six interwoven stories paint a picture of an American criminal justice system gone horribly wrong and six brave souls who persevered to survive it. "The #1 play of the year…intense and deeply affecting…" –*NY Times.* "Riveting. Simple, honest storytelling that demands reflection." –*A.P.* "Artful and moving…pays tribute to the resilience of human hearts and minds." –*Variety.* "Stark…riveting…cunningly orchestrated." –*The New Yorker.* "Hard-hitting, powerful, and socially relevant." –*Hollywood Reporter.* [7M, 3W] ISBN: 0-8222-1946-8

★ **STRING FEVER by Jacquelyn Reingold.** Lily juggles the big issues: turning forty, artificial insemination and the elusive scientific Theory of Everything in this Off-Broadway comedy hit. "Applies the elusive rules of string theory to the conundrums of one woman's love life. Think *Sex and the City* meets *Copenhagen.*" –*NY Times.* "A funny offbeat and touching look at relationships…an appealing romantic comedy populated by oddball characters." –*NY Daily News.* "Where kooky, zany, and madcap meet…whimsically winsome." –*NY Magazine.* "STRING FEVER will have audience members happily stringing along." –*TheaterMania.com.* "Reingold's language is surprising, inventive, and unique." –*nytheatre.com.* "…[a] whimsical comic voice." –*Time Out.* [3M, 3W (doubling)] ISBN: 0-8222-1952-2

★ **DEBBIE DOES DALLAS adapted by Erica Schmidt, composed by Andrew Sherman, conceived by Susan L. Schwartz.** A modern morality tale told as a comic musical of tragic proportions as the classic film is brought to the stage. "A scream! A saucy, tongue-in-cheek romp." –*The New Yorker.* "Hilarious! DEBBIE manages to have it all: beauty, brains and a great sense of humor!" –*Time Out.* "Shamelessly silly, shrewdly self-aware and proud of being naughty. Great fun!" –*NY Times.* "Racy and raucous, a lighthearted, fast-paced thoroughly engaging and hilarious send-up." –*NY Daily News.* [3M, 5W] ISBN: 0-8222-1955-7

★ **THE MYSTERY PLAYS by Roberto Aguirre-Sacasa.** Two interrelated one acts, loosely based on the tradition of the medieval mystery plays. "… stylish, spine-tingling…Mr. Aguirre-Sacasa uses standard tricks of horror stories, borrowing liberally from masters like Kafka, Lovecraft, Hitchcock…But his mastery of the genre is his own…irresistible." –*NY Times.* "Undaunted by the special-effects limitations of theatre, playwright and *Marvel* comic-book writer Roberto Aguirre-Sacasa maps out some creepy twilight zones in THE MYSTERY PLAYS, an engaging, related pair of one acts…The theatre may rarely deliver shocks equivalent to, say, *Dawn of the Dead*, but Aguirre-Sacasa's work is fine compensation." –*Time Out.* [4M, 2W] ISBN: 0-8222-2038-5

★ **THE JOURNALS OF MIHAIL SEBASTIAN by David Auburn.** This epic one-man play spans eight tumultuous years and opens a uniquely personal window on the Romanian Holocaust and the Second World War. "Powerful." –*NY Times.* "[THE JOURNALS OF MIHAIL SEBASTIAN] allows us to glimpse the idiosyncratic effects of that awful history on one intelligent, pragmatic, recognizably real man…" –*NY Newsday.* [3M, 5W] ISBN: 0-8222-2006-7

★ **LIVING OUT by Lisa Loomer.** The story of the complicated relationship between a Salvadoran nanny and the Anglo lawyer she works for. "A stellar new play. Searingly funny." –*The New Yorker.* "Both generous and merciless, equally enjoyable and disturbing." –*NY Newsday.* "A bitingly funny new comedy. The plight of working mothers is explored from two pointedly contrasting perspectives in this sympathetic, sensitive new play." –*Variety.* [2M, 6W] ISBN: 0-8222-1994-8

DRAMATISTS PLAY SERVICE, INC.
440 Park Avenue South, New York, NY 10016 212-683-8960 Fax 212-213-1539
postmaster@dramatists.com www.dramatists.com

NEW PLAYS

★ **MATCH by Stephen Belber.** Mike and Lisa Davis interview a dancer and choreographer about his life, but it is soon evident that their agenda will either ruin or inspire them—and definitely change their lives forever. "Prolific laughs and ear-to-ear smiles." *–NY Magazine.* "Uproariously funny, deeply moving, enthralling theater. Stephen Belber's MATCH has great beauty and tenderness, and abounds in wit." *–NY Daily News.* "Three and a half out of four stars." *–USA Today.* "A theatrical steeplechase that leads straight from outrageous bitchery to unadorned, heartfelt emotion." *–Wall Street Journal.* [2M, 1W] ISBN: 0-8222-2020-2

★ **HANK WILLIAMS: LOST HIGHWAY by Randal Myler and Mark Harelik.** The story of the beloved and volatile country-music legend Hank Williams, featuring twenty-five of his most unforgettable songs. "[LOST HIGHWAY has] the exhilarating feeling of Williams on stage in a particular place on a particular night…serves up classic country with the edges raw and the energy hot…By the end of the play, you've traveled on a profound emotional journey: LOST HIGHWAY transports its audience and communicates the inspiring message of the beauty and richness of Williams' songs…forceful, clear-eyed, moving, impressive." *–Rolling Stone.* "…honors a very particular musical talent with care and energy… smart, sweet, poignant." *–NY Times.* [7M, 3W] ISBN: 0-8222-1985-9

★ **THE STORY by Tracey Scott Wilson.** An ambitious black newspaper reporter goes against her editor to investigate a murder and finds the *best* story…but at what cost? "A singular new voice…deeply emotional, deeply intellectual, and deeply musical…" *–The New Yorker.* "…a conscientious and absorbing new drama…" *–NY Times.* "…a riveting, tough-minded drama about race, reporting and the truth…" *–A.P.* "… a stylish, attention-holding script that ends on a chilling note that will leave viewers with much to talk about." *–Curtain Up.* [2M, 7W (doubling, flexible casting)] ISBN: 0-8222-1998-0

★ **OUR LADY OF 121st STREET by Stephen Adly Guirgis.** The body of Sister Rose, beloved Harlem nun, has been stolen, reuniting a group of life-challenged childhood friends who square off as they wait for her return. "A scorching and dark new comedy… Mr. Guirgis has one of the finest imaginations for dialogue to come along in years." *–NY Times.* "Stephen Guirgis may be the best playwright in America under forty." *–NY Magazine.* [8M, 4W] ISBN: 0-8222-1965-4

★ **HOLLYWOOD ARMS by Carrie Hamilton and Carol Burnett.** The coming-of-age story of a dreamer who manages to escape her bleak life and follow her romantic ambitions to stardom. Based on Carol Burnett's bestselling autobiography, *One More Time.* "…pure theatre and pure entertainment…" *–Talkin' Broadway.* "…a warm, fuzzy evening of theatre." *–BrodwayBeat.com.* "…chuckles and smiles of recognition or surprise flow naturally…a remarkable slice of life." *–TheatreScene.net.* [5M, 5W, 1 girl] ISBN: 0-8222-1959-X

★ **INVENTING VAN GOGH by Steven Dietz.** A haunting and hallucinatory drama about the making of art, the obsession to create and the fine line that separates truth from myth. "Like a van Gogh painting, Dietz's story is a gorgeous example of excess—one that remakes reality with broad, well-chosen brush strokes. At evening's end, we're left with the author's resounding opinions on art and artifice, and provoked by his constant query into which is greater: van Gogh's art or his violent myth." *–Phoenix New Times.* "Dietz's writing is never simple. It is always brilliant. Shaded, compressed, direct, lucid—he frames his subject with a remarkable understanding of painting as a physical experience." *–Tucson Citizen.* [4M, 1W] ISBN: 0-8222-1954-9

DRAMATISTS PLAY SERVICE, INC.
440 Park Avenue South, New York, NY 10016 212-683-8960 Fax 212-213-1539
postmaster@dramatists.com www.dramatists.com

NEW PLAYS

★ **INTIMATE APPAREL by Lynn Nottage.** The moving and lyrical story of a turn-of-the-century black seamstress whose gifted hands and sewing machine are the tools she uses to fashion her dreams from the whole cloth of her life's experiences. "…Nottage's play has a delicacy and eloquence that seem absolutely right for the time she is depicting…" –*NY Daily News.* "…thoughtful, affecting…The play offers poignant commentary on an era when the cut and color of one's dress—and of course, skin—determined whom one could and could not marry, sleep with, even talk to in public." –*Variety.* [2M, 4W] ISBN: 0-8222-2009-1

★ **BROOKLYN BOY by Donald Margulies.** A witty and insightful look at what happens to a writer when his novel hits the bestseller list. "The characters are beautifully drawn, the dialogue sparkles…" –*nytheatre.com.* "Few playwrights have the mastery to smartly investigate so much through a laugh-out-loud comedy that combines the vintage subject matter of successful writer-returning-to-ethnic-roots with the familiar mid-life crisis." –*Show Business Weekly.* [4M, 3W] ISBN: 0-8222-2074-1

★ **CROWNS by Regina Taylor.** Hats become a springboard for an exploration of black history and identity in this celebratory musical play. "Taylor pulls off a Hat Trick: She scores thrice, turning CROWNS into an artful amalgamation of oral history, fashion show, and musical theater…" –*TheatreMania.com.* "…wholly theatrical…Ms. Taylor has created a show that seems to arise out of spontaneous combustion, as if a bevy of department-store customers simultaneously decided to stage a revival meeting in the changing room." –*NY Times.* [1M, 6W (2 musicians)] ISBN: 0-8222-1963-8

★ **EXITS AND ENTRANCES by Athol Fugard.** The story of a relationship between a young playwright on the threshold of his career and an aging actor who has reached the end of his. "[Fugard] can say more with a single line than most playwrights convey in an entire script…Paraphrasing the title, it's safe to say this drama, making its memorable entrance into our consciousness, is unlikely to exit as long as a theater exists for exceptional work." –*Variety.* "A thought-provoking, elegant and engrossing new play…" –*Hollywood Reporter.* [2M] ISBN: 0-8222-2041-5

★ **BUG by Tracy Letts.** A thriller featuring a pair of star-crossed lovers in an Oklahoma City motel facing a bug invasion, paranoia, conspiracy theories and twisted psychological motives. "…obscenely exciting…top-flight craftsmanship. Buckle up and brace yourself…" –*NY Times.* "…[a] thoroughly outrageous and thoroughly entertaining play…the possibility of enemies, real and imagined, to squash has never been more theatrical." –*A.P.* [3M, 2W] ISBN: 0-8222-2016-4

★ **THOM PAIN (BASED ON NOTHING) by Will Eno.** An ordinary man muses on childhood, yearning, disappointment and loss, as he draws the audience into his last-ditch plea for empathy and enlightenment. "It's one of those treasured nights in the theater—treasured nights anywhere, for that matter—that can leave you both breathless with exhilaration and…in a puddle of tears." –*NY Times.* "Eno's words…are familiar, but proffered in a way that is constantly contradictory to our expectations. Beckett is certainly among his literary ancestors." –*nytheatre.com.* [1M] ISBN: 0-8222-2076-8

★ **THE LONG CHRISTMAS RIDE HOME by Paula Vogel.** Past, present and future collide on a snowy Christmas Eve for a troubled family of five. "…[a] lovely and hauntingly original family drama…a work that breathes so much life into the theater." –*Time Out.* "…[a] delicate visual feast…" –*NY Times.* "…brutal and lovely…the overall effect is magical." –*NY Newsday.* [3M, 3W] ISBN: 0-8222-2003-2

DRAMATISTS PLAY SERVICE, INC.
440 Park Avenue South, New York, NY 10016 212-683-8960 Fax 212-213-1539
postmaster@dramatists.com www.dramatists.com